W9-BNR-221

YOU ARE *More* THAN YOU KNOW

FACE YOUR FEARS, FIND YOUR STRENGTHS

PATSY CLAIRMONT

WORTHY
PUBLISHING

Copyright © 2015 by Patsy Clairmont

Published by Worthy Books, an imprint of Worthy Publishing Group, a division of Worthy Media, Inc., One Franklin Park, 6100 Tower Circle, Suite 210, Franklin, TN 37067.

WORTHY is a registered trademark of Worthy Media, Inc.

Helping people experience the heart of God

eBook available wherever digital books are sold.

Library of Congress Control Number: 2014957121

All rights reserved. No portion of this book may be reproduced, stored in a retrieval system, or transmitted in any form or by any means—electronic, mechanical, photocopy, recording, scanning, or other—except for brief quotations in critical reviews or articles, without the prior written permission of the publisher.

Scripture quotations marked NKJV are taken from the New King James Version®. Copyright © 1982 by Thomas Nelson. Used by permission. All rights reserved. Scripture quotations marked NIV are taken from THE HOLY BIBLE, NEW INTERNATIONAL VERSION®, NIV® Copyright © 1973, 1978, 1984, 2011 by Biblica, Inc.® Used by permission. All rights reserved worldwide. Scripture quotations marked NASB are taken from the NEW AMERICAN STANDARD BIBLE®, Copyright © 1960, 1962, 1963, 1968, 1971, 1972, 1973, 1975, 1977, 1995 by The Lockman Foundation. Used by permission.

Patsy Clairmont is represented by Mike Atkins Entertainment, Inc.

ISBN: 978-1-61795-325-5 (trade paper)

Cover Design: Studio Gearbox
Cover Image: © onimages/Veer
Interior Design and Typesetting: Christopher D. Hudson & Associates, Inc.

Printed in the United States of America
16 17 18 19 VPI 9 8 7

Tell me, what is it you plan

to do with your one wild

and precious life?

—Mary Oliver

CONTENTS

INTRODUCTION

Boo!

Fight your fears and you'll be in a battle forever. Face your fears and you'll be free forever.

—Lucas Jonkman

S he is such a happy soul."

"He's so dear."

They sound like tidy descriptive packages but then, truth be known, Ms. Happy Soul turns out to be an uptight tyrant at home and Mr. Dear turns out to have scary secrets including a second family tucked away in another town. No one can be easily described nor can we be counted on to always be just one way. We are far too complicated to fit into a pithy phrase.

Have you ever tried to draw a picture of your emotional life? Instead of using a straight-edge ruler to help illustrate who we are inside, we probably would be more accurately represented by a map, perhaps the one that shows Paul's shipwrecks, beatings, and prison visits or the journey of the Israelites on their way to the Promised Land. What looked like it should have been a short jaunt over to the land of milk and honey ended up being a forty-year escapade of ups and downs—enemies, celebrations, battles, and fears. This truly is a more accurate visual of the twists and turns within us as well as the road ahead of us.

Little has changed since that Exodus walk. We are still going through emotional ups and downs. We are still in a mind war with an adversary who'd like to take us out. We continue to have

3

seasons of joy, though never long enough from our vantage point. And we are still dueling with fear.

The National Institute of Mental Health claims that there are 6.3 million people who have been diagnosed with a phobia. And that's just the ones who have sought help. They also tell us that 60 percent of things we fear never happen. Golly, that seems like a waste of our energy, doesn't it? Fear takes effort to sustain and leaves us depleted. I should know. I was an agoraphobic and found myself housebound and at times bedbound with exhaustion from maintaining a fear-based life. My exaggerated emotions backed me into a suffocating place and under the influence of fear. My passion for life had turned to apathy, which led to an emotional and mental paralyzation. I couldn't seem to see past my fear.

In the children's movie *Monsters, Inc.*, monsters like Sulley and Mike counted on fear to power their city, Monstropolis. So they would sneak into children's bedrooms to scare them into a scream by creeping out of closets, crawling under their beds, and peeking through windows. The vibrations of the screams were then captured and turned into electrical energy to power their city. But much to the monsters' amazement, they discovered that a child's love and laughter offered them even more of what they needed. It was a greater force than fear. And they realized that their own fear of children was unfounded. So the monsters began sneaking into the kids' rooms and doing silly things to get children to laugh.

I like that concept because it's true—love and laughter are a powerful force. And a good belly laugh massages our inward parts, which causes our blood pressure to balance, our circulation to improve, our attitudes to adjust, and our angry defenses to come down. It clears the cobwebs from our brains, as well as myriad other health benefits. More times than I can count in our fifty-plus years of marriage, my ire has dissolved into a puddle of giggles because of my husband's ability to make me laugh. What a gift!

But life is not always fun or laugh-worthy or easily solved, like when we were kids and our parents would chase our fears away by their very presence. Today our grown-up fears tend to loom like Goliath and stick with us like a bad cold.

Unfortunately our true "monster" enemy, Satan, is not impressed with our capacity for laughter because fear is one of his strongest weapons against us. He knows it squelches our humor, intimidates us, and weights our heart. I have found laughter to be one of our stronger defense weapons against angst since a burst of guffaws relaxes muscles and releases life-giving endorphins. So we have this push-pull between us and the one who wants to dull our existence and annihilate our faith if not our life.

The first time we hear fear speak in the Bible is through Adam in the Garden of Eden after he and his wife gave into the seductive temptation and sin of eating from the tree of the knowledge of good and evil (Gen. 2:16-17). God called to Adam, "Where are you?" Adam responded, "I heard Your voice in the garden, and I was afraid . . . and I hid myself" (Genesis 3:9-10). Never before had fear been a part of their relationship equation. Our all-knowing God knew where they were and what they had done, but he asked Adam to put him into a place of ownership of his choice. God continues to do that throughout Scripture with his people, for in ownership and repentance comes liberty and dignity.

The day came in my life when I had to answer the same question as Adam: "Patsy, where are you?" And my response reverberated with familiarity: "I was afraid and I hid."

Coming out of my hiding places and facing my fears has taken years, and on some days I continue to scramble up mountains with scraped knees and slide down into valleys with a thump. I'm on my way to the Promised Land, but it's obvious I'm not there yet. There are still days I need a hand-up from another journeyer. And there are still days I want to hide, since every season of life brings its set of threats, yet because of God's mercy and grace, I press on.

Perhaps one of my steps to recovery thus far will help you with scary feelings that are part of your struggle. God does that. He uses broken people to help broken people. We are not too far gone or too complicated or too hidden that God cannot find us, help us, and hear our deepest cry. He knows the monsters under our bed and is not the least bit rattled.

In the pages ahead we will talk about ways that help us deal more effectively with our sometimes shaky psyche. We may be uptight with tension, numb from denial, or down in the dumps with sadness. God has designed us to be capable, functional, joyful, and ingenious. Add to the mix sane, sensible, and stable. Yes, you. And me. We are truly more than we know.

I am not a professional counselor. I am a seasoned girlfriend (full of age) and a cheerleader to those who are tied up in knots. If someone were to ask me if I were brave, my knee-jerk response would be, "Heavens, no!" But the truth is I'm far braver than I knew when I was in hiding. I never dreamed that just ahead of me was a life of stage work, writing, art, and travel. I was in my late twenties the first time I flew. My knees were bruised from knocking, but God would use that trip to open the world to me in a way I never imagined.

Every time I stepped through a fear, I experienced deeper liberation. Facing fears tutored me in growing stronger, and that's when and how I learned I am more than I know. The same holds true for you. And the reason we are more than we know is because the Lord is greater than we can search out in our lifetime. We cannot mentally or imaginatively contain God because of his "more-ness," which is why we need faith to make the leap between our limitations and his limitlessness. Gratefully, Christ offers to companion us every step of our journey.

We may be uptight with tension, numb from denial, or down in the dumps with sadness. God has designed us to be capable, functional, joyful, and ingenious. Add to the mix sane, sensible, and stable. Yes, you. And me. We are truly more than we know.

We have no idea what God has planned for us just beyond our fear, but I guarantee it will be a life-expanding adventure full of meaning. So bring your journal, your camera, your binoculars, and a magnifying glass . . . there's plenty to discover in God's Word, applaud in your life, and celebrate together.

Deliberate on . . .

"For God has not given us a spirit of fear, but of power and of love and of a sound mind" (2 Timothy 1:7 NKJV).

Discuss . . .

- Are you brave? Give an example.
- Name two fears you have that go "boo" in the night.
- Do you laugh often, occasionally, or seldom?

1

Keep Pedaling

Promise me you'll always remember: You're braver than you believe.

—A. A. Milne

thought learning to ride my new bicycle would be facing my greatest fear. I was nine years old and it was tall and I was not. While reluctant to initiate actual moving contact with my bike I was overjoyed to receive it. But then it's one thing to have something in one's possession and another to own it in the sense you actively embrace its purpose. I dreamt about it though. In my dreams I beat all the neighborhood kids in speed races while my ponytail stood straight out behind me like a raccoon's tail in gale force winds. Truth, though, was my legs were short—which prevented any official speed records because I was too busy trying to keep the metal contraption upright while my ponytail slapped me silly as I gyrated from side to side. Eventually I conquered my fear of falling by learning to toe-tap the petals as they spun, which kept the bicycle moving fast enough to keep it and me from crashing.

Life soon taught me much bigger lessons about fear and falling as I felt like a flea perched on the edge of an eagle's wing swooping above Kilimanjaro. In reality though, all five feet of me was tucked inside a basket held aloft by hot air (not mine) that pulsated inside a balloon suspended over the Maasai Mara in

Africa. Below us, elephants stampeded. Honest. I really couldn't make this up. Not about me.

If you had known me as a young adult, you would not have believed that I, Ms. Anxiety, would allow myself to be put in that kind of intimidating scene. Ever! Oh, who am I kidding? If you had met me *last week* you would have been suspicious! I tend to be skittish and verbal about heights and falling. Besides, I'm resistant to handing over the "steering wheel" of my life to anyone.

And get this: When I asked the hot-air-man, who was steering the wicker crate, what his name was, he replied, "Moses."

"Moses!" I squealed. "You've got to be kidding! Why, you didn't even make it to the Promised Land and you're driving my basket?"

To which he announced, "We will be crashing soon."

Oh, yes he did.

"Listen, Mo, don't say the word *crash* even as a joke," I insisted.

"Oh, it's no joke," he assured me. "We have little to no control when the basket collides with the earth. We just bounce along with it until it comes to a stop." A wry grin seemed to catch the edge of his mouth, as though Moses enjoyed this information.

(It seemed to me as though this data should have been offered to the participants prior to boarding.)

Any man who will say the words *crash* and *collide* to a former agoraphobic as we dangle in mid-air obviously has abandonment issues and was left far too long to bob about in the Nile. It suddenly occurred to me that all that separated me from a free fall were a few ropes and a deflatable balloon.

A vivid picture of us landing amidst a hungry pride of lions and being pounced upon filled the screen of my mind. Fear does that. It rushes in and paints boldly on our vulnerability in hopes we'll subscribe to fear's next scary edition.

And my reaction might have been more inflated, if there had been time. Except suddenly, as Moses had predicted, we crashed and bounced until we skidded to a stop. Quite jarring. We crawled out. No lions in sight. There was just a distant herd of great horned beasts and a skulking hyena who surveyed our arrival with disdain.

Once my feet were planted on terra firma where I felt a tad more in control, I liked Balloon-Moses way better. But then I've always been drawn to Moses. Not the hot air one, but the wilderness Moses. The Bible one who, against all odds and his own wild fears, lived to view the Promised Land.

It is through the rigors of God's people and the frailty of their humanity, that we will take our own skittering pulse. Because, lets face it, life can be scary. 9/11 scary. Tornado scary. Pain scary. Job-loss scary. War scary. Death scary. Yada, yada scary.

And it's the "yada, yada" fears I want to focus on—those that loom large in our eyes, or even the ones we cannot see yet. The unfamiliar noise in the night, the breaking-news report, the approaching-storm warnings, the aging process, etc. It's my belief and experience that if we can handle the daily fears, we will be better prepared to deal with the more profound fears. Although any little fear can potentially morph into a biggie when we are in the struggle. Symptoms tend to magnify their threat via emotional intensity conveying danger in the moment.

Like the time I was at a friend's house in the Deep South . . . think Texas deep. I was walking through the kitchen when I realized there was a sizable scorpion on the wall. Yes, a scorpion. How do you spell *s-c-r-e-a-m*?

My hosts had retired for the evening several hours prior, so to actually scream seemed inappropriate, if not ungrateful. Packing my bags and calling a cab was an option, but my dilemma was they had two young children and I felt responsible to do something with this hostile critter so that they were not left in harm's way. While I don't have arachnophobia (fear of spiders), neither do I have warm fuzzies for anything that can send me rushing to the nearest emergency room.

It's my belief and experience that if we can handle the daily fears, we will be better prepared to deal with the more profound fears. Although any little fear can potentially morph into a biggie when we are in the struggle.

In the "moment," that Texas creepy crawler appeared to be the size of a dinner plate and its arched tail looked like a cannon. I searched about looking for a weapon. I thought, *Dynamite . . . shotgun . . . jackhammer*. But all I could find was a mason jar, a paper plate, and a coffee cup. Then I had a come-to-Jesus talk with myself, followed by some mental cheerleading. "C'mon, honey, you are way bigger than him. *Weigh* bigger!" Yes, I meant to spell it that way. "You can do this!" I said in a whimper.

My hands were shaking, my heart was doing the butterfly stroke, and sweat had reached the top of my knee socks. Then suddenly I reacted. I trapped him with the jar against the wall, scraped him down inside the jar with the plate, and cov-ered the jar with the plate, setting the coffee cup on top as an anchor.

Whew! Done.

Well . . . almost.

My body wasn't finished reacting. My heart ricocheted off my tonsils, my body tremors vibrated my headscarf, and my socks squished with each step I took. I double-checked my prisoner—okay, triple-checked—to reassure myself of its secure entrapment and then went to bed. That night I awoke frequently to check the walls and my bed for creepy crawlers.

The next morning I anticipated a medal from my hosts for my heroic combat, but instead I got a shrug and a smile. Seems scorpions are no big deal when you face the enemy on a reg-ular basis. (FYI: I'm almost certain someone had shrunk the scorpion . . . he didn't look anywhere near as gargantuan in the light of day. And the cannon on his rear-end had shriveled into a derringer.)

I didn't know when I first saw the scorpion that I could handle him all by myself. In fact, I was certain I couldn't. And I wouldn't have tried if I could have figured another way out. But what a relief afterward when I realized I did it.

Little me tackled a new fear and *won*. I had more courage than I knew.

As I said, while I am not arachnophobic, I was an *agora*phobic—afraid of open spaces and crowds of people. Although I would argue that by the time I was housebound I had collected many more fears than just spaces and people . . . fears that short-circuited my freedom and fried my reasoning skills.

I was afraid of doctors, hospitals, medicine, elevators, heights, tunnels, bridges, people's opinions, just to name a few. Fear does to us what I did to the scorpion . . . it traps us and makes our world smaller. And then it sends scary messages to our brain, setting off seismic physical reactions, which have the potential of creating an environment of internal terror.

Here's the good news: Just as there is a way into the cycle of paralyzing fear, there is a way out of the intimidating labyrinth.

Fear suggests that it came on suddenly when actually it's been setting up housekeeping inside of us most of our lives. Satan has just been waiting for a situation where he would catch us off guard and set off fear explosives.

If you are bound up in fear that keeps you from living life to its fullest, I want to say that it is possible to one day go on safari to a far land, dangle in a hot-air balloon over stampeding animals, and lasso scorpions as a pastime.

If you are bound up in fear that keeps you from living life to its fullest, I want to say that it is possible to one day go on safari to a far land, dangle in a hot-air balloon over stampeding animals, and lasso scorpions as a pastime.

You may be thinking, *I'd be happy to just be more functional with the freedom to come and go in my life without the shadowed companion of anxiety in tow.* I understand. I remember when my prayer was to simply get to the grocery store and back home again without a panic attack.

I couldn't imagine how delicious freedom would be, how wide the door would open, or how far around the globe it would take me. I didn't know . . . God's expansive heart.

Was it (recovery) fast? Nope. Was it easy? Not for *moi*. Has it been worth it? Oh, glorious world and darling people, yes, yes, *yes!*

Oh, wait . . . am I saying I never have to battle my way through anxiety? Of course not. But therein lies the liberty . . . now I know how. It doesn't trap me or hold me prisoner as it once did. Nor does it threaten me with isolation and incrimination.

The reason is that I discovered the startling truth: We are more because God is more than we can even imagine . . . and He created us with unending potential.

As we grow stronger mentally, it helps us to balance emotionally. And while it is a journey toward mental, emotional, and social harmony, gratefully there are many spectacular views along the path whether pedaling on our bike, in an aerial basket, or afoot. As we take hold of this understanding, we become calmer, hopeful, and much more joyful.

We are a virtual surprise party waiting to celebrate. Just about the time we think we know ourselves, we do or say something that startles or even impresses us. Right?

It's because *we are more than we know*. (Yes, I'll be saying this often.) I believe if we can grasp even a speck of God's greatness it will free us from fighting for control wherever we find ourselves.

Deliberate on . . .

> "So if the Son makes you free, you will be free indeed"
> (John 8:36 NASB).

Discuss . . .

- What promotes your inner harmony? (e.g., music, quiet, certain people)
- Do you believe you are more than you know? (e.g., braver, smarter, sturdier)
- In your words, describe God's expansive heart.

2

Okay Queenie, Hand Over the Scepter!

Be not angry that you cannot make others as you wish them to be, since you cannot make yourself as you wish to be.

—Thomas à Kempis

C ontrol is such a stir stick. We think, if we have it, we will feel safer, steadier, and saner so we fight for it like our kingdom depends on it. But truth is, in this life, we are in control of very little.

For instance, take . . . the weather, the economy, our health, people's opinions, their actions, traffic (eek!), history, hormones (double eek!), tomorrow, ten minutes ago, etc. See what I mean?

Life is unruly. Like my hair, which has thinned, fuzzed up, and turned many shades of white and gray with streaks of blonde and brown. Good gravy, Gertie, what's that about?

My mom lived to be eighty-eight and her hair was a sandy blonde, period. My grandmother who lived to be ninety-seven had gray hair, end of story. While mine is a wad of indecision, like the price of real estate.

And real estate is what we are after with our control issues . . . right? We want to know that our kingdom is under our reign. We want to have the ultimate say-so over our acre of life. We'd appreciate some royal respect and acknowledgement when we raise our scepter.

In my twenties, I tried desperately to regain a sense of being in charge of my acre after experiencing a series of panic attacks.

Try as I might, though, I continued to feel intimidated and threatened by almost everything and everyone. These feelings did not align themselves with royalty.

I was hyper-vigilant, concerned someone or something would push a hidden button that would trigger panic in me. I didn't understand what was making my body turn against me nor did I know how to make peace with my taunt emotions. So I withdrew from society and took refuge in my home and eventually my bed. I felt as if I were in exile.

A panic attack causes adrenaline to shoot through our bodies like a high-speed sprinkler system, which puts us into both flight and fright reactions. Our heart pounds, our body has tremors, our eyes lose focus, we break out in sweats, we feel nauseous, we struggle to breathe, and our thoughts spin. And that's just for openers.

It took me years before I figured out what I'm about to tell you. Maybe I wasn't ready until then for the personal responsibility it would require of me. I'm not sure. But one thing I know, when I learned this truth, it saved me from a life of acute anxiety.

Here it is . . . God created our will to be stronger than our emotions, so that when our feelings are unreasonable, inaccurate, or out of control, we don't have to become a victim of their intensity. We can choose to be brave and take deliberate steps toward health and balance.

God created our will to be stronger than our emotions, so that when our feelings are unreasonable, inaccurate, or out of control, we don't have to become a victim of their intensity. We can choose to be brave and take deliberate steps toward health and balance.

Our Creator designed us with a will so we can override our frenzied feelings and set our mind to live the best version of who he intended us to be. Yes, even in the midst of emotional and mental derision. Not as queens but as servants.

That is a simple truth, but it becomes difficult to execute during an inner, symptom-ridden, emotional tirade. Believe me, I know. I remember when anxiety episodes caused my hands to shake with tremors, my eyes would lose focus, and my breaths came in short gasps. At that point, my skimpy determination would fizzle and fear would escalate.

Determination to be well is a good place to begin change, but that alone is not enough. It needs to be backed up with a mental and emotional plan that aligns itself with God's counsel.

The truth is, we can do it. Honest. Ask me. I'm the girl who went from a vow to spend my life hiding in my bed to eventually become the woman who has hot-footed it back and forth across America and beyond for almost four decades speaking to literally millions of women.

I am a member of five airlines' frequent flyer clubs. I'm a Flying Colonel on one airline and a two-million-mile card holder on another. The point is, I get around.

So I believe it is possible to discover a plan that will allow you to lead a life full of meaning and adventure. For me, it didn't happen all at once.

Think . . .

Baby steps.

Delays.

And emotional sticky wickets.

At least that's what it felt like when I was involved in the demanding work of getting well. For me it was the hardest work I had ever done. I found that to override unhealthy emotions takes focus, determination, and energy. It also takes the help of others. We weren't meant to do this life alone.

Let me say, *practice* matters when implementing a new survival plan. *Progress* matters as well, because it's a way to measure our success of implementing our strategies. But watch out for the stumbling block of *perfection*.

Satan is a rock thrower bent on our ruination, and the rock of perfectionism is one of his favorite projectiles to hurl. He knows that when it hits, it will bruise and lacerate us with shame, discouragement, and hopelessness.

Satan does not fight fair. His intention is our destruction. His language is lies. Carefully crafted lies to fit inside our vulnerability.

But God is invested in our ongoing welfare. He speaks of peace, love, and "more." So to live in God's provision of inner resting places, and to not be seduced, deceived, or intimidated by the enemy, we have to be savvy to God's counsel and how to integrate it into our lives. Conquering fear is our God-given right. He empowers us to win.

The reason we are more than we know is because God is greater than we can imagine.

Read that again.

It's the last half of that sentence—*because God is greater than we can imagine*—that we need to lean into before we can embrace the first half. Otherwise we think we are the big deal, which is ego-hype that sets us up for a fall. But understand that it is the greatness of our God and his generosity that gives us worth, meaning, and a powerful future, and it is Christ who carries us even in our weakness.

God is in control. Isn't that a relief . . . at least most of the time? Like managing the solar system, maintaining the earth's alignment, and lighting the stars? Yes, I think we'd all agree that he who created the heavens and the earth should also manage them. But the closer his control comes to our life—especially when it's going differently than we imagined—the more we tend to react against it. It's not easy to release our grip on our imaginary scepter.

Let's face it . . . it's hard to let go. Let go of fears, offenses, children, unfulfilled dreams, youth, health, influence, perceived rights, et cetera, et cetera, et cetera. Oh, the endlessness of et cetera!

Some years ago our oldest son Marty was in a coma for twenty-one days as a result of pneumonia and the H1N1 virus. Believe me, I wanted to instruct God on the outcome. Instead, as the doctors informed me daily that Marty probably would not survive, my main prayer was one word: *mercy*. I repeated it often. Over Marty, over my husband, and over myself as well. Somehow that prayer bathed me in peace as I let go and waited on the will of God. I was deeply grateful Marty survived. I believe, though, had he died, God would have met us in our loss as well. The word *mercy* holds no power in itself; it's the act of relinquishment that helps us to accept God's decision even when we don't understand it.

It takes more than a casual curtsy or head-tip toward God's sovereignty to let go; it will take a face on the floor, heart-cry of relinquishment before most of us tend to hand over our scepter.

It takes more than a casual curtsy or head-tip toward God's sovereignty to let go; it will take a face on the floor, heart-cry of relinquishment before most of us tend to hand over our scepter.

I know it did for me. Handing it over is just the first step, which will have to be repeated again and again because we forget again and again who is ultimately in charge.

Believing in God's good intentions toward us and Christ's abundant provisions for us makes relinquishment a safer choice. Yet when hardships come or panic initiates we tend to doubt that God's heart is truly for us. While that is a human reaction it is also the soil that the enemy looks for to sow seeds of inner discord.

Handing it over is just the first step,
which will have to be repeated again
and again because we forget again and
again who is ultimately in charge.

Satan wants us to believe we are not loved or provided for. He wants us to believe we are orphans rather than heirs. He wants us to live like victims rather than conquerors. But the stronghold of fear can be broken, and our freedom begins as we say yes to all God has for us.

Let's say "yes" out loud right now. Really . . . out loud. Seems almost silly and too simple, but *yes* is a powerful word that can align our hearts with God's will. (Nothing silly about that.) And hearing our self in agreement with his plan strengthens our commitment to his outcome.

I try to begin every morning with a *yes* to God. I believe it's the most profound prayer we can offer.

Yes, God, I believe in you.

Yes, God, I acquiesce to your sovereign care.

Yes, God, I trust your heart and your plan.

Yes, God, I acknowledge that you have designed me to be more than I know.

Rehearsing who God is promotes hope in our hearts and reminds us that God is greater—*so* much greater—than we can imagine.

So am I saying to those of us who live with our lives in knots, if we hand over control, that—*voila!*—we are good to go? The answer to that would be "no." In fact, we may have to hand control back over to the Lord many times in a day. Some of us are so entrenched in our controlling behavior that we don't recognize it for what it is.

My control was often couched in "concern" for others . . . especially my husband and children. I remember when a farmer friend of ours wanted to take our then-young son for a ride on his tractor. I imagined every tractor accident I'd ever heard about and decided it wasn't a good idea. So while my husband and I went to the store our friend took him out on the tractor anyway. To make matters more tense, our friend then put our son on his horse, which I would have never allowed, and led him around the farm. (Our friend was an experienced farmer with a truckload of grandchildren.)

I arrived back at the farm as the farmer was lifting our boy off the horse. Now we had two people with control issues butting heads—our friend and me.

Was he right to disregard my wishes? No. Was it healthy for me to base my choices on fear? No. But I confess, it was easy for me to get wrapped up in "How dare he?" as a way to avoid looking at the root of my choice. My fear was being passed on through my control, and our friend could see that. While it wasn't his place to step in, I must admit I'm grateful he did . . . for our son's sake. (Besides, what's a godfather for?)

Ask God to begin showing you where your "concern" for others is actually your fear coming out as control. It's time to lay down our scepters and relinquish our rights to be in control.

Deliberate on . . .

"Trust in the Lord with all your heart

and lean not on your own understanding;

In all your ways submit to him,

and he will make your paths straight"

(Proverbs 3:5-6 NIV).

"But whoever listens to me will dwell safely,

And will be secure, without fear of evil"

(Proverbs 1:33 NKJV).

Discuss . . .

- When do you tend to pull your scepter of control out?
- Do you see a relationship between control and fear? Explain.
- Write a prayer of relinquishment.

3

Mother, May I . . . ?

*It's okay to realize that you
are crazy and damaged
because all of the best
people are.*

—Anne Lamott

I remember as a kid that I loved to play hopscotch, but somehow in my neighborhood that invariably led to the game of "Mother, May I?"—a game in which I never felt a smidgen of control. A game I lost again and again. Even when I was given three giant steps, my short legs didn't take me far. I always lagged behind long-legged Cheryl who could, in one stride, leave me in her chalk dust. I tended to give up quickly and feel hopeless far too soon. My mantra became, "I'll never win. I'm too little. Why even try?" Words that would not serve me well in the years to come.

By the time I was a young adult, I had given up and given in to agoraphobia. Emotionally, I was so far behind anyone I knew that there wasn't even a puff of dust in sight. I knew of no one who struggled with paralyzing fears and physical drama as I did. I truly believed I was the only one who had crazy episodes and for sure the only oddball who had to be rushed to the hospital for Demerol for my panic attacks. I had mentally given up and had decided I'd probably spend the rest of my life in bed.

So imagine my surprise and relief when, in a moment of desperation, I found a support group for anxiety patients through my medical doctor and risked attending a meeting. Something

I've read many times was definitely true for me back then: The moment you're ready to quit is usually the moment right before the miracle happens. (My husband waited for me in the parking lot in case I needed a quick way of escape. He felt it was a small price to pay if it meant I would get help for my bizarre and demanding behavior.)

The participants quietly gathered in the basement of a church, and I couldn't believe it—each one of them appeared normal. That was a relief since I was certain any group who used the term *mental health* would look, well, mental. After observing just one meeting, I never had to have Demerol again. I'm not kidding. No more fast trips to the ER. One meeting . . . that's all it took. That, my friend, is the power of hope.

Knowing I wasn't the only one in a mental muddle and that others had found a way to survive their panic gave me a possible path out of my despair. To hear their stories, well, it gave me the courage to tell the truth about my own. Their newly learned reactions to the tensions in life helped me to set a different standard for my behavior. They felt like I did, nervous and intimidated, yet they were functioning. Hearing them made me feel braver, and they taught me by example that I didn't have to feel courageous to take scary life-giving steps. They weren't playing childish games with their mental health; they were determined to get well.

The group had guidelines on how to share their struggles and discomfort lest we rattle off our woes and depress each other. We weren't allowed to complain during meeting time, only report. This was a critical change-point for me; I had made a career of whining. I never had verbal guidelines, at least not ones I followed. I felt you wouldn't understand how bad my situation was if I didn't explain it in vivid word pictures. Yes, I was a full-time actress. I didn't realize this exaggerated tendency was often the stick that stirred up my issues and kept my fear recycling. I was actually promoting the scary feelings that surged through me.

I had been waiting to be rescued. I didn't realize I held the keys toward my own recovery and it would begin as I limited my barrage of words, monitored my thought life, and exercised my will to make new choices.

To change ingrained habits will take knee-knocking gutsy effort. And personal mercy.

I love this quote from Dorothy Bernard, the late actress from the silent movie era: "Courage is fear who has said its prayers." You have to become your own cheerleader. It's not easy when you have spent years saying mean-spirited things to yourself to then attempt being kind-spirited and tender-hearted.

To change ingrained habits will take knee-knocking gutsy effort. And personal mercy.

I had to give up calling myself stupid, dumb, and ugly every time I made a mistake or passed a mirror. I learned that continuing to use those and other cruel words was like holding a lit match to my tissue-paper emotions.

Also, defeatist phrases such as "I will never be any different" and "I can't" were full of failure that doused my hope of getting well. Eliminating those trigger phrases helped open up a path past the blockade of my own bleak attitudes.

I believed many things about myself, others, and God that just weren't true. But they felt like gospel to me. You see, *lies nest inside beliefs*. For instance, I thought God had favorites and I wasn't on the list. I believed no one could like me for me, that I would always need to try to be someone I wasn't. And I believed most people were conniving and couldn't be trusted. I misjudged people because I measured them against my own undeveloped heart.

I had to learn that feelings aren't facts. That lies wedge inside of beliefs and emotions to distort and corrupt them. A tactic of the enemy of our soul whose goal is to rob and destroy our hope, faith, and well-being. During my panic, the enemy would hiss these lies:

"This is the worst panic you have ever had."

"You are going to lose control."

"You are losing your mind."

"You are going to die."

"You will never get well."

You have to become your own cheerleader.
It's not easy when you have spent years saying
mean-spirited things to yourself to then
attempt being kind-spirited
and tender-hearted.

God didn't design emotions to think for us, and I slowly began to understand I couldn't depend on mine for accurate information, especially as reactive, sad, and sick as they were. They needed to be on hiatus, while my mind-set shifted to a better place.

Gratefully God gave us brains that could be reasoned with and instructions in Scripture on how our minds would best operate. I noticed that as my thoughts became steadier from the kind discipline of meditation, that my emotions became less volatile and overwhelmed. I needed to place my mind in the gentle comfort of the Psalms, the firm instruction of the Proverbs, and the life-giving mercy of the Gospels.

Scripture tells us to bring "every thought into captivity to the obedience of Christ" (2 Cor. 10:5 NKJV). Now that's not easy because our minds are busy about many things. Mine, I'm sure, looked like a pinball machine on tilt; bells ringing, lights flickering, and coins pinging. I found that to get to a healthier, saner pattern of thinking I needed the mental supervision of God's scrutiny. Even today, decades after my initial recovery, if I'm not faithful in allowing God's Word to permeate my mind, I can fall prey to negative and disturbing thoughts.

So how did I work on my thought life? The same way I do today. I study and memorize Scripture to renew my mind. Once I get a truth in my memory then I try to live that truth to the best of my understanding, asking God to guide me. In the early years of my struggles, I stumbled around in my awkward attempts, but gradually I became more positive, less critical,

Father Daughter
Ball 2016

Ted Harlow

0-1219560
50 M6 ?

more loving, less argumentative, more calm, and less frantic. I learned I could break my habit of making everything sound like a catastrophe by neutralizing my words, which in turn helped calm my emotions.

At first the changes in me seemed miraculous, because I went from hiding in my bedroom to attending a group meeting. That, in itself, was more than we (family, friends, doctors) thought was possible because I was so depressed, fearful, and convinced I was hopeless. Progress became visible when I began taking personal responsibility for my responses toward others instead of blaming. I was becoming more reasonable and less reactive.

The support group helped me stay on track and gave me the mental tools to brave getting back into the main stream of life. They taught me how to self-monitor my reactions to stress, and how to manage my physical and emotional responses through *will training.*

I had no idea that I could command my muscles to move and that they would obey, even when my emotions were throwing a hissy-fit inside of me. I found I could *will* myself to sit quietly when my *feelings* were insisting I flit around like a distraught June bug. I could hold my tongue (who knew?) even when stinging words like angry wasps were buzzing in my head.

I could will myself to get out of bed even when my body felt like lead weight.

God created us with a sturdy will of choice. We can choose to conduct ourselves differently than we feel. What a liberating truth!

It sounds like a no-brainer, that our will is stronger, but try to convince yourself to be reasonable when every emotional siren in you is screeching *emergency!* I needed to give my emotions a time out, while I got my head on straight. My emotions were infected and affected by false information and negative thoughts; they needed the regular healing influence of truth and love along with the structure of discipline to help rein them in.

I found that the less I gave into my negative feelings and the more I lived God's principles, my life became bearable, as did I. I gradually was able to go off my tranquilizers (four a day), cigarettes (two packs a day), and coffee (potfuls a day . . . yes, pots).

I am not against medication; in fact, I celebrate the provision it can be for there are many who have need of the balance it offers—hormonally, chemically, and physically. Unfortunately many people have suffered terrible relational side effects from drugs, as Wendell Berry suggests: "People use drugs, legal and illegal, because their lives are intolerably painful or dull. They hate their work and find no rest in their leisure. They are estranged from their families and their neighbors. We need drugs, apparently, because we have lost each other." But even more, we have lost sight of ourselves.

Our frantic pace keeps us running toward a goal we can't quite define instead of resting in the definition of who God made us to be—productive, peace-based people with a divine sense of destiny. We can't outrun ourselves. Our untended heart will spill out in ways we had not meant it to. We are invited to enter green pastures of goodness and mercy, for it's in the presence of Christ and under his tutelage that we are assured of our worth.

We can't outrun ourselves. Our untended heart will spill out in ways we had not meant it to. We are invited to enter green pastures of goodness and mercy, for it's in the presence of Christ and under his tutelage that we are assured of our worth.

Connecting in life-changing ways with others was healing for me; like opening a window in a stuffy room. I could breathe again. Having a "neighborhood" in my life was one of the ways

God showed me his constancy. Randy Frazee wrote in *The Connecting Church*:

> Two television shows, *Seinfeld* and *Friends*, consistently received the top awards from the People's Choice Awards. . . . What both shows have in common is a small group of friends that go in and out of each other's lives and apartments spontaneously more times in a half hour than most "real" Americans experience in a year. . . . (I)t was about a group of friends spending lots of spontaneous time together, talking about every day stuff and loving every minute of it.

God knew we would need companions on the journey, ones that wouldn't take giant steps away from us and leave us in their dust, but would link arms for the walk home.

Deliberate on . . .

"Now behold, two of them were traveling that same day to a village called Emmaus . . . and they talked together of all these things which had happened. So it was, while they conversed and reasoned, that Jesus Himself drew near and went with them" (Luke 24:13-15 NKJV).

Discuss . . .

- When is the last time you felt Jesus near to you?
- What does Scripture say about his ongoing presence in our lives?
- Who is in your "neighborhood"?

4

The Gift of Denial

The human mind isn't a
terribly logical or
consistent place.

—Jim Butcher

My husband, Les, grew up in the wild woods of the Michigan's Upper Peninsula with his parents, four brothers, and a sister. Copper Harbor, a remote vacation village on Lake Superior, was a regular stomping grounds for their motley crew who spent a good portion of their lives tromping through the woods. Their dad was the owner of a lumber camp, before he drank it away, so the kids grew up tree and wildlife savvy.

Well, sort of.

Les tells stories, of him and his brothers, when they chased bears out of the woods so tourists could take pictures of the wildlife. Can you spell *e-e-k*? I mean, one bear-paw pivot and those boys would have been in serious trouble; as in Kibbles 'n Kids. The brothers had enough firsthand experience as young trappers and hunters to know you could not trust the disposition of a skunk, much less a bear. But they believed they could handle it . . .

Which brings us to the subject of denial.

I believe many of us would not have survived our childhoods without it. Think about it. Often we weren't equipped as a child to know how to process the things going on around us, in us, and to us. So we boxed up our fears and confusion and tucked it deep into the shadows and pretended what we couldn't understand or process didn't happen. But sometimes it grumbled under our bed at midnight as a monster or peeked in our bedroom windows as a bully bandit or hissed like a snake in our nightmares. It came out in our behavior—head banging, nail biting, bed wetting, painful shyness, sleep walking, etc. As we got older it affected our thoughts about the world and influenced our personal theology, though we seldom realized it. We dragged oddities into our adult life that came out in exaggerated fears, obsessive behavior, sarcastic wit, and myriad other ways.

It's not until we reach our adult life that most of us begin to sort out how past life events impacted us mentally, emotionally, physically, and socially. This usually requires us to drag out our musty box of denial and risk opening it to the air and light.

If you have a trunk load of sad or scary memories you may need help to lug it out and sort through it. Memories are infused with old feelings and can rush at us, like a bear, with intimidation, while dismantling our emotional sense of security. Wisdom says invite a seasoned soul to stand with us when we open our box so we don't feel alone (isolation is one of the enemies tactics), plus having a wise journeyer with us can help us maintain perspective. It may be a counselor or a trusted loved one, just make sure it's someone you feel safe with and who has come far enough in their own journey that they know how to encourage you.

If you have a trunk load of sad or scary memories you may need help to lug it out and sort through it. Memories are infused with old feelings and can rush at us, like a bear, with intimidation, while dismantling our emotional sense of security.

Here's some advice for selecting the right person, though: Seldom is our best friend a good choice as a guide since we usually align ourselves with those who are broken and stuck in similar ways as ourselves, so their insight can fall short of our need or theirs. But they make great prayer people because they love us and want the best for us. If they don't want the best perhaps we should rethink why we would walk closely with someone who is not tender-hearted toward us.

Remember, the enemy slips lies into our most vulnerable moments, so when we've grown up believing a lie from childhood, it feels true. My husband grew up believing he should have been able to rescue his mother from the violent treatment of his father. The truth being Les was a child and could not have stopped his raging dad from his brutal behavior, but the enemy seeded Les's young emotions with shame, responsibility, and guilt.

Les spent years after that trying to rescue every sad soul he met as a type of repentance for what he couldn't do for his mom. His regrets lacked discrimination because they were based in the childhood lie that he was to blame for what his dad did. And while it is kind to be compassionate, it is unproductive and unwise to rescue people who need to take responsibility for their own behavior.

I was one of those dysfunctional souls that Les repeatedly tried to rescue. I often felt and behaved helpless and hopeless, but remember feelings are not facts. I was not incapable, but I was both uninformed and misinformed. I lived like all feelings were gospel, which was how I ended up in self-inflicted isolation. And with Les willing to do for me what I should have been doing for myself I became not only emotionally sick but emotionally selfish.

They (I'm not sure who "they" are, but it appears there are a lot of them) say we marry one of our parents, usually the one we have the most unresolved issues with. For Les, I represented his mom's desperate neediness, so I was someone he could try to rescue. But I also was his dad, with my unpredictable, demanding behavior. I single handedly had recreated Les's childhood home atmosphere. Of course, I didn't realize it nor was Les cognitively aware that our unhealthy home environment felt familiar to him and therefore was "normal." Norms can be riddled with dysfunction, but because they are what we have known there is a sick safety in it.

It was when I began making steps of progress toward change and recovery, that we ran into new sets of challenges between us. While Les was relieved I wasn't such a handful to deal with, he also started to feel his own emotional lies confront him. Because if I didn't need him to constantly rescue me then what did that say about his worth as a husband and a man? How could he meet his quota of rescues that his unrelenting guilt required of him?

Les was conditioned from his home life to unpredictability and desperation, he wasn't prepared for the unfamiliarity of balance and safety that was slowly being established in our home with my recovery. So we went from me being dramatic to him being disruptive in his attempt to reinstate his "normal," which was chaotic and tension filled. (Remember even unhappiness feels comfortable if it's all we've known.)

My progress became part of his undoing. This eventually put Les in the position of having to pull out his trunk of denial and look at the lies in his belief system. What a relief when the cloak of childhood shame, that should have never rested on him, was removed from his shoulders. And likewise, what liberation for Les when the lie, that he was responsible for my well-being, choices, and behavior, was broken. Les learned he could be lovingly supportive, while allowing Jesus to be my ultimate Rescuer. And he grew to have a genuine compassion for the frightened child inside of him, who would have rescued his mom if he could have.

Also we both learned as long as we were busy telling the other one what he should do we weren't taking responsibility for our own behavior. We have come a long way in our relationship and yet in a snap we fall back into old patterns. So we both have to work at maintaining order, peace, and civility, so our marriage can prosper. Fifty-two years of marriage and we are still having to make concerted efforts to be grown up. But, you know what? Flourishing love is a worthy goal.

The enemy would use denial as a way to keep us trapped in childhood pain, while the Lord uses it to help us survive in this broken world until we are in a place to face the truth and then take new steps of growth.

Yes, denial is a gift.

To pull the rug of denial out from under someone can be both terrifying for them and cruel. Too much light at one time can be blinding. We can cause others to cower deeper into the darkness. We should not try to be someone else's conscience. There's only one Holy Spirit and he knows how and when to nudge us into the light of conviction so it can lead to deliverance.

In the beginning of creation God spoke "good" over us. And he still does. His intentions are always based in love. He warns us that we live in a fallen world, but one day redemption will come and the earth and his people will be as he had originally planned. Until then he promises to use all things for good for those who love him.

Just because we can clearly see what seems obvious to us in someone's life, doesn't mean they are even slightly aware of it, or that God has called us to be his mouthpiece in this matter. I have more than once driven a wedge between me and someone else by my tendency to blurt out a truth that the recipient was not prepared to hear, and I have on a number of occasions had others do that to me.

Giving up denial is a risk, but one that allows us access to who we were meant to be (instead of who we are afraid we might be). And it frees us of misconceptions that we have to constantly be guarded and defensive, because behind guarded is the belief that we are in control of our own destiny. Grasping the revelation of God's sovereignty, to the degree we can, brings internal relief as we understand more fully his *protection*, his divine *plans*, his holy *provisions*, and his active *presence* in our lives.

The question that floods our minds is this: If God loves us why does he allow injustice, violence, illness, and trauma to touch our lives? In the beginning of creation God spoke "good" over us. And he still does. His intentions are always based in love. He warns us that we live in a fallen world, but one day redemption will come and the earth and his people will be as he had originally planned. Until then he promises to use all things for good for those who love him. I don't understand exactly how that works, but belief isn't based on my ability to reason out God; faith is trusting what I can't see. And quite honestly I often can't see what he's up to, but then he's not accountable to me; I am accountable to him.

We don't look back to blame others for their humanity or ours. (Don't get stuck in the muck of blame. Instead, become a humble recipient of mercy and truth.) We look back to be freed from anything that distorts our concepts of who we are and who God is. We don't want childish beliefs and the enemies lies to keep us from the "more" of today and from a confident future.

Deliberate on . . .

". . . that Christ may dwell in your hearts through faith; that you, being rooted and grounded in love, may be able to comprehend with all the saints what is the width and length and depth and height—to know the love of Christ which passes knowledge; that you may be filled with all the fullness of God" (Ephesians 3:17-19 NKJV).

Discuss . . .

- How has denial worked in your behalf?
- How has it hampered your growth?
- What does God's sovereignty mean to you?

5

Taskmaster Friend

*True freedom is impossible
without a mind made free
by discipline.*
—Mortimer J. Adler

My mom was a taskmaster . . . or so I thought when I was a kid. Don't most children? Like wearing boots and shoes during the winter. I thought barefoot and snow held far more appeal and adventure. Today I understand she was trying to prepare me for life. Real life, where we do what we need to do to take care of our responsibilities and become contributing adults. But my mom didn't start a work regime with me until I was a teen, which was a little late, and it didn't take. I had grown accustomed to her doing for me what I should have been learning to do for myself. By the time I turned seventeen I was self-indulged, depressed, and a new wife unequipped for life. Yes, I married at seventeen. And by twenty I was floundering as a first-time mom who couldn't get her act together. I didn't know how to manage my time, my emotions, or my thought life.

When things swirl around in your head and life feels like a free fall, sometimes you need to take charge and be tough with yourself—not mean, but definitely firm. (And by firm, I mean when you give yourself an assignment, you do it—even if you don't feel like doing it!)

By the time I wobbled my way into a get-well plan, I needed *firm*. I had coddled my emotions for so long they didn't know what was good for them or how to behave. My emotions needed boundaries. It was obvious that I had to get my brain back in charge of decision making and my emotions back to the feeling work they were designed to do.

In the beginning of growing healthier, I would mentally pack up my feelings and picture myself putting them on a shelf. I would tell them as I walked away, "I'll be back for you later." My goal wasn't to lose touch with how I felt; I just wanted to temporarily deny my emotions control over me. I was learning to exercise my will and move my muscles toward life-giving actions. Like getting out of bed.

Training your will requires one's brain to be engaged, and as you, like me, have probably experienced, emotions aren't big on reasoning. I had stockpiled many fears, and most of them weren't rational. Do you remember the game Ms. Pac-Man? Well, I felt like my emotions were winning as they grew bigger and bigger from gobbling up my brain cells . . . which would have been fine if the emotions were joy instead of despair.

People often ask me the difference between a phobia and a fear. I tell them we have stepped into the territory of phobia when our fear grows to the point we allow it to dictate our choices and we rearrange our lifestyle to accommodate it. And while my answer may be a simplification of a complicated issue, it helped me to differentiate what I should or should not allow to influence my decision making.

Here's an example: When I was struggling with debilitating anxiety, every time there was even the hint of a storm approaching I was certain I would be swept away in it. It was irrational. (Not that it couldn't happen, but really, what were the chances?) I was certain God was out to get me. And that was irrational, too. (I knew he didn't want to get me; he wanted to love me.) These fears led to extreme actions during bad weather threats. I would anxiously listen to every weather report I could find on the radio and television. I would pace from window to window for hours, looking for signs of impending doom. I would insist my husband come home from wherever he was to be with me. Often I couldn't sleep or eat until the storms were past.

Now, I've been in a few truly rugged storms in my life and it makes sense to take shelter and be aware of the threat they present. But I panicked if even a dark cloud rolled overhead and dribbled a little rain. I planned every outing around the weather, even simple trips to the grocery store a mile away. My fear had become a phobia ruling my behavior and the quality of my existence.

I began to improve when I deliberately studied and meditated on God's immutable love, which helped me tear down the lie that he was "out to get me." And I practiced not working myself up by refusing to window peer, pace, or listen to repeated weather reports. When thoughts and habits feed our fears, trust me, they grow more demanding.

It was "taskmaster" work not to give in to my emotions, when they ranted, "You are in danger!" Discipline is not easy to implement when your fear is tap dancing on your brain. But, usually, the hard work of change takes place in the scary trenches.

I would have to will myself to sit quietly and think on things that were calming. I would record on cassette tapes (yes, it's been a while) peace-giving verses from Scripture and life-enhancing chapters from books. Then instead of giving into the "pace and fret" routine I had created, I'd listen to them. I'd clean out a messy drawer to distract myself or I'd bake a pie so I had a positive/visible result from my efforts.

One particularly disconcerting season I baked so many pies we couldn't eat them all! I realized I was getting obsessive when we were offering free pies to anyone who came to our door, including the mailman. I remember he looked at me befuddled and then looked at his mailbag, as if to say, "And just where do you think I should put it?"

It's not unusual for fear-based people like myself to give up one unproductive habit just to replace it with another. But quite honestly, every improved upgrade is a good step toward better mental health. To have a pie to offer someone after a storm was a great improvement over developing yet another ulcer. My positive pie tangents were helping me take steps away from my negative worry routine.

It's not unusual for fear-based people like myself to give up one unproductive habit just to replace it with another. But quite honestly, every improved upgrade is a good step toward better mental health.

In our early years of marriage my husband had a propensity to drink too much beer. Since his father was an alcoholic, we both knew this was not a good habit for him, lest he repeat his father's legacy. I'm sure living with my dysfunction didn't help Les, but two addicted people does not a good home make. I was strung out on fear and he was escaping through alcohol.

After a particularly rough patch of his drinking Les suddenly quit, which is not how it usually happens. But then he began drinking excessive amounts of sodas. Yet even though they can be bad for our health, it was still an upgrade. When he polished off a six-pack of cola he could still walk a straight line and he didn't have a hangover. Yes, definitely an upgrade.

So during our recovery as individuals, and as a couple, if you stopped by for a visit we could have offered you a slice of pie and a soda to chug it down. Your blood sugar would have soared, but I wouldn't have been pacing and peering and Les wouldn't have been tipsy. I'm sure our recovery looked awkward to onlookers, but we knew we were making progress.

I'm reminded to be cautious judging other people's habits . . . because, I know from experience, they could be worse.

I'm told that we addictive-type personalities want to cover our pain, so we use food, spending, sex, drugs, sleeping, gambling, alcohol, work, people, blame, social activities, the Internet, etc., to distance and disguise what we don't know how to solve inside of us. The problem is, addictions only temporarily placate and then we need more, more, and more to help distract us and soothe our unsettledness.

For me, giving up my cigarettes, which had progressed to two packs a day, was an important step because the amount I smoked escalated with the level of stress I was feeling. I came to a place I wanted to trust the Lord with my needs, instead of rushing to a habit that was bad for my health. And I wanted to be a better example for our son.

I'm told that we addictive-type personalities want to cover our pain, so we use food, spending, sex, drugs, sleeping, gambling, alcohol, work, people, blame, social activities, the Internet, etc., to distance and disguise what we don't know how to solve inside of us. The problem is, addictions only temporarily placate and then we need more, more, and more to help distract us and soothe our unsettledness.

During my withdrawal, to say I was cantankerous would be kind. I did not transition sweetly, but I did make it, and eventually became tolerable again. God bless those who helped me through that season with their many kindnesses.

And then I lived happily ever after . . . not.

I started eating too much. That's what we do if we deal only with the addiction and not the pain. We do the old switcheroo. Then I traded eating too much for watching too much television, and then I was shopping too much, and so on. It wasn't until I began taking my mental, emotional, and spiritual health seriously that I passionately pursued my faith walk.

I searched God's Word and I looked for books on how to mature. I read voraciously, I circled lines that spoke to me, memorized quotes, and I talked to insightful people about what I had read. I attended conferences and I spent endless hours in conversation with my pastor and his wife who were fresh out of seminary and eager to share.

I worked hard to encircle myself with believing friends. I sat under every good teacher I could find at churches, retreats, camps, and home gatherings. I listened to taped messages and radio pastors. Some of my favorites in those formative years were Corrie ten Boom, Jill Briscoe, Charles Swindoll, and Jill Renich, just to name a few. They were truth tellers and pointed their readers toward Christ with practical insights for change.

I would tell my friends how I felt and they would tell me what God's Word said about my feelings. That way I could decide if I wanted to align my head and heart with God's will or limp along as I was. The more truth I embraced the better I felt about myself, my marriage, and my mothering. Slowly my pain began to siphon off, which then made room inside me for God's truth to counsel me even more deeply. Did I say slowly? I wondered if I'd ever be fit for human consumption. I was so splintered. Gratefully the Lord is in the business of integration. He's an expert on mending broken people.

Relationships were hard for me. I was either way too quiet or way too chatty. Usually I erred on the side of nervous chatty, the kind where you don't breathe lest someone else gets to talk. I was full of thin opinions, which didn't fare well with folks. And some say I was bossy. Oh, wait, that was last week. I tell you, some habits keep popping back up. Have you noticed that—in yourself?

I also had a sarcastic streak in me that, once unleashed, could be cruel. Not a good way to build loving relationships.

However, I learned that my sarcasm was a defense mechanism I used when I felt hurt, threatened, judged, jealous, rejected, or misunderstood. And what sounded funny to some was laced with biting anger toward others. To temper this habit (and, may I add, character flaw), I had to learn to correctly identify what

I was feeling, own those feelings, and take responsibility by obeying God's directives.

Instead of hiding behind sarcasm, if what I was really struggling with was resentment or jealousy, I needed to face it, confess it, and ask God to heal my heart so I could be more loving and less vindictive. I often had to also confess to the ones I'd been harsh with and ask their forgiveness. Not an easy task for a willful person but, when accomplished, helped me to soften my responses.

May I just say the sarcasm habit has taken years to dismantle? I'm still tempted to hide there in certain circumstances. Actually I've found many of my old ways are willing to be reinstated in a moment's notice with my permission. So to combat the temptation to revert to harmful habits, I have to guard my heart and mind by girding them up with truth. I have to guard my mouth by practicing silence. And I have to guard my choices by purposing to take a higher path.

Don't be downcast if you, too, keep messing up. Humanity is such an untidy condition . . . for all of us. That's why Christ provided forgiveness and mercy. We can, with the empowering of the Holy Spirit, maintain a supple spirit by acknowledging who is in charge and bending our knee to the redemptive name of our Savior.

There's a reason God tells us to wear battle armor; we are on guard duty, but we are not alone. Christ and the Holy Spirit join us on patrol. We won't finish up the fight against our tendencies or the enemy until glory, so anticipate the battle.

Humanity is such an untidy condition . . . for all of us. That's why Christ provided forgiveness and mercy. We can, with the empowering of the Holy Spirit, maintain a supple spirit by acknowledging who is in charge and bending our knee to the redemptive name of our Savior.

But there is good news: when our will becomes a holy taskmaster, led by the Spirit, our emotions can take their proper place to serve us and others well. So if you have indulged your emotions and need corrective guidelines to help you gain a healthier lifestyle, turning your heart toward God, first, in prayer, and then in a willingness to take the next step of obedience, is a great place to begin.

Two years ago a heavy box full of kitchenware fell on my foot fracturing it in two places. I wore a Velcro foam boot on that foot for months as my injury healed. I thought I'd never get out of it. I had to go to physical therapy, do exercises, and follow strengthening guidelines. My physical therapist at times seemed more like a taskmaster when the recovery exercises became painful. Gradually, though, my injuries healed and now I can tap dance . . . well, almost.

Hang in there with your journey, it might be painful, challenging, and tedious, but doing the next right thing can bring you seasonally from a fierce winter into a flourishing spring.

Deliberate on . . .

"I have told you these things, so that in me you may have peace. In this world you will have trouble. But take heart! I have overcome the world" (John 16:33 NIV).

Discuss . . .

- Do you need to get tough with yourself?
- Where might you begin . . . and when?
- What battle gear will you rely on (e.g., helmet, breast plate, sword, etc.)?

6

Boundaries

No is a complete sentence.

—Anne Lamott

A place to begin to live a more disciplined and loving exis-tence is with two powerhouse words that when harnessed can serve us well in that goal: "yes" and "no." They are the "stop" and "go" lingo that we use daily, but often it seems we are unsure which one is appropriate. Otherwise, why is it that one of our leading health issues is stress? Wouldn't it make sense that if we were yes-ing and no-ing correctly, our stress levels would be in a much better place? We'd know how to take care of ourselves and we wouldn't allow our insecurities or peoples' opinions to dictate our choices.

Have you noticed we tend to be "yes" people to our friends and "no" people to our children? At least when they are young. Or was that just me?

I think the "no" to my kids was a habit rather than a thought through directive. It often just seemed easier to whip "no" out of my mommy purse than to get more involved with a "yes" that might include driving them somewhere, packing up overnight paraphernalia, or adding someone else's children to our fam-ily parade. Then one day a mom with more life experience said to me, "Say 'yes' to your children as often as is appropriate so that when you do have to say 'no' it has impact." That helped me to listen more closely to my children's requests and not to just throw a "no" out to have it over with. Sure enough, it worked—at least most of the time.

But maybe from the get-go you were a "yes" mom, afraid you'd have to bear your children's displeasure and disrupt your need to maintain peace. So you spent a great deal of your energy trying to keep them happy, only to discover the little darlings had an insatiable appetite to be entertained, which kept you hopscotching across town.

Can I just say, balance is fragile. So hard to attain and even more difficult to maintain. Too much weight on either end of the teeter-totter and down we go. Splat!

The rules for "yes" and "no" changed in my mind from a child to an adult. A "no" to adults seemed, well, a tad rude . . . and might put us in the position of being judged as wrong, unfriendly, or—worse!—un-Christlike. So some of us have said "yes" to things that we should never have agreed to. Things that required our energies to the point we had nothing left to invest in our families by the time we dragged our sorry selves home. This "yes" depletion sets us up for resentment, exhaustion, and leaves our priorities all lopsided. (Which is why Anne Lamott said, "'No' is a complete sentence," in one of her Facebook posts.

It's okay to say "no" and not feel you have to defend or explain why. It is enough that you know you are doing what is right for you and your family.)

Depletion is just the beginning of the teeter-totter tumble.

For me, learning girlfriend boundaries has been hard work. I didn't want people to feel rejected or offended by my "noes," so I have often nodded my head when I should have shook it. I have been a poor boundary maker because I was a poor boundary keeper. In fact, I hardly knew I was trampling over people's wishes, because I measured their preferences by my own. But my preferences were steeped in my neediness and were as off-centered as my phobic lifestyle had been, so I didn't realize how far I was from a norm. Unless someone spoke up, I didn't realize I had invaded their space by my needy ways, nor did I realize that they had rules I was unaware of, like, "Call before you come over."

I was raised by open-armed Southerners who had an open-door policy. "Y'all come here," was our household mantra. I figured that was how the whole world operated. If you were in my neighborhood, I thought surely you'd stop in and I took it personally if you didn't. If I was near your house, I just knew you'd want me to drop in. You can only imagine how often that was an issue for others.

I gradually learned that my need for the constant company of others was my attempt to feel accepted, included, and served as a distraction from my own brokenness. It was a way to briefly escape myself. But distractions are temporary and therefore soon leave us clamoring again for relief.

Let me just say, if you have a hole in your heart and you are seeking for other people to fill your neediness, it doesn't work that way. Jesus is our need meeter and he's a jealous God who isn't going to allow us to have our deep needs met by others. Believe me, I tried. People can add to our joy, but they can't be our source of joy. People can encourage us, but they can't be our Wonderful Counselor. People can contribute to our wholeness, but they can't be our core. Christ has reserved that place for himself.

How do we know if we have holes in our heart? This is my guideline: if we have a pulse in our wrist we have a hole in our heart. By virtue of our being alive in this fallen world, we have been hurt and we have hurt others. We all need Jesus. Jesus redeems us from a destiny of separation from God. He is literally the bridge over the troubled water within us. Christ positions us in a place of divine favor by cleansing us from our sin, empowering us for our new life, and interceding on our behalf.

He heals our broken places, which is a lifelong process of learning and growing in love and understanding.

Jesus is our need meeter and he's a jealous God who isn't going to allow us to have our deep needs met by others. Believe me, I tried. People can add to our joy, but they can't be our source of joy. People can encourage us, but they can't be our Wonderful Counselor.

A friend told me that when she encountered Christ, her atheistic beliefs crumbled and her heart found purpose and hope. She had wrestled previously with her temper and a sarcastic mouth, but after becoming a Christian, she lost her anger. It just disappeared. A couple years later, she found it again and she wondered what that meant about her faith.

It's true that our "yes" to Jesus is when our new life begins, but it doesn't mean we are delivered from our humanity. Our tendencies toward anger, spitefulness, jealousy, envy, etc., will be a temptation as long as our spirits are wrapped up in these earth suits we wear. Once we take our last breath on earth, our human boundaries are cast aside and our life in eternity begins . . . a life free of all hostile encumbrances.

Until then we have the capacity to please and honor God by following Christ in what we do, which also leads to our ongoing integration. God is the therapist who "invented" the concept of boundaries, starting in the garden. He immediately established the boundary Adam and Eve were not to cross, eating from the tree of the knowledge of good and evil, and what the consequences would be if they did. And his follow-through was swift.

It's true that our "yes" to Jesus is when our new life begins, but it doesn't mean we are delivered from our humanity. Our tendencies toward anger, spitefulness, jealousy, envy, etc., will be a temptation as long as our spirits are wrapped up in these earth suits we wear. Once we take our last breath on earth, our human boundaries are cast aside and our life in eternity begins . . . a life free of all hostile encumbrances.

The Lord knew, because of our sin-tendencies, we would need guidelines and consequences. He didn't establish them to be unkind, but to protect us from the enemy and our own weaknesses.

"Yes" and "no" play a huge part in our maturity. They are grown-up words that involve our participation.

"Yes," is a word often equated with popularity and promotions, while "no" can be thought of as unfriendly and uncooperative. The bottom line is not even how overcommitted we are, but which answer is Christ-directed for our life at the time we are asked. Busy or bored, we were not meant to say "yes" to all invitations, or "no."

Recently I was asked to audition for a small role in a Christian movie. I was ecstatic for the opportunity and jumped at the chance. I was interviewed and read lines for the director over Skype, and a couple days later I received a thumbs up. But after mulling it over more carefully, I realized the timing couldn't have been worse for me or my husband and that I should not have been so eager before weighing the cost. So I had to back-track and do a lot of apologizing.

If there is a reluctance in our heart about our answer, when possible, we need to put time between us and our decisions. Often just saying, "Let me get back with you," will give us the space we need. That way we don't have regrets *and* we don't inconvenience others.

Saying "yes" when we should say "no" or saying "no" when we should say "yes" is often fear-based. We fear being misunderstood, rejected, judged, or never asked again, so we answer according to our insecurities. Or we fear taking steps out of our comfort zone to risk the unknown. Fear is tricky; it wears many disguises. It can sound compassionate and practical, convincing us that our motives are pure, while all the time that devil-rascal is pushing us deeper into the shadows of doubt, apathy, and confusion.

Saying "yes" when we should say "no" or saying "no" when we should say "yes" is often fear-based. We fear being misunderstood, rejected, judged, or never asked again, so we answer according to our insecurities. Or we fear taking steps out of our comfort zone to risk the unknown.

I remember the first time I stepped out of my agoraphobic lifestyle to attend a weekend women's retreat. I had a list of reasons I couldn't go that sounded convincing to me, but my friend MaryAnn knew I would be skittish. So she said, "I'm going to ask you something, but I don't want you to answer me." I thought,

How odd! But I agreed not to say a word in response. "Would you like to attend a weekend ladies retreat with me?" she asked. I remained silent but my head was already saying "no." "Here's what I want you to do," she continued. "First, when you hang up, I want you to pray and ask God to guide you in the answer. Second, I want you to ask your husband what he thinks. Then decide."

I agreed, though I knew God would not think it was a good idea, because I was still too emotionally fragile for that kind of escapade. And I knew my husband would not want me to venture off that far without him, given my history. But I had promised to pray first and then talk to Les, so I did.

Had you been listening in to my prayer, I'm afraid you would have heard me instructing the Lord. "Lord," I said, "I know you don't want me to go to this event in my condition." Then I listed my frailty in detail in case he had forgotten. Then the strangest thing happened. No bells from heaven, no iridescent lights off angels' wings, or rolling thunder, but I became very uncomfortable. Very. It was the kind of discomfort that made me feel as if he was about to say, "Go."

I made a beeline for my hubby to protect me from such a directive. I didn't tell Les I had prayed first or my feeling that

God was about to ask me to do something I wasn't emotionally prepared to do. Instead, I told him that the invitation would require me to stay two overnights on the other side of our home state of Michigan. Les had never heard of a retreat where thousands of women talked about God all weekend, and since he had not yet invited Christ into his life I knew it probably would spook him. I thought that would work to my advantage.

Les listened carefully, asked me several questions in regard to location and dates, and then said, "I think you should go." I was speechless. I think what silenced me was, it sounded as if God and my husband were on the same page and, for me, that was startling.

Les and God were the two I ran to in my panic and insecurity and they were saying, "Go." How could this be? They both knew better than to think I could do this. It would require me to ride several hours away from my safe people and safe place. There would be thousands of women gathering and I hadn't done crowds in years. I was unfamiliar with the program so there were many unknowns, which left room in my imagination for the enemy to play volleyball with my fears.

In the weeks preceding the retreat I thought of a thousand reasons why I couldn't go, but they all crumbled in front of me.

Retreat day arrived and MaryAnn pulled up to my house to find me red-eyed and trembling, but she appeared not to notice my swollen face from crying nor the panic in my anxious eyes. I had my tranquilizers in one hand, my cigarettes in the other, my Bible under my arm, and off we went.

And. My. Life. Changed. Forever!

God captured my attention and affection that weekend and lit a passion in me for his will, his word, and his ways. I came home a different woman . . . still very broken, but definitely on the mend.

Obviously that retreat was not an easy "yes" for me, but a very important one. The enemy would love to have persuaded me to stay in the "safety" of my familiar fears. But MaryAnn, God, and Les had other ideas. It was a divine collusion to over-throw the grip of the enemy on my life.

Following that retreat weekend inspired by my bold new steps of growth, Les said a life-changing "yes" to Christ. As he puts it, "Patsy, when you changed I knew there had to be a God." That's one advantage to being as broken as I was: when I changed, God got all the credit. Anyone who had known me knew I didn't have it in me to be different or brave. We were all about to find out, though; I was more than we knew because God had plans.

Remember: When people ask you to do something you are unsure of, tell them you'll get back to them, then pray, and if you're married get your spouse's input. Time and counsel are wise components to help you give the right "yes" or the right "no." It will add to your maturity and make your life far less stressful and complicated. It positions you to have a say-so in the quality of your life.

Deliberate on . . .

"But let your 'Yes' be 'Yes,' and your 'No,' 'No.' For whatever is more than these is from the evil one" (Matthew 5:37).

Discuss . . .

- When was the last time you said a firm "no"?
- Is your tendency to be a "yes" girl or a "no" girl?
- Is there someone with whom you need to establish new boundaries? How will you do that?

7

Hole in Your Bucket

God uses cracked pots.

—Patsy Clairmont

F or a while there was a teaching story that circulated on the Internet about water pots and how one pot had a hole in the bottom and day after day, as it was carried to a village, it dribbled water out on the dusty trail. This wasn't helpful to the bearer of the pot since every drop was life-giving moisture that was seeping away, but later it was discovered that new life was sprouting forth on the now-moist path because of the unintentional daily watering the splatters offered.

We, like the marred pot, because we are imperfect, have the potential to offer through our brokenness life-giving moisture to others in the form of hope. That's exciting! But every story has two potential sides. While our brokenness can, under the redemptive plan of God, be used for good, it is also an ongoing loss for us if we don't deal with our jaded responses to our pain, which can cause our sense of value to seep out. Facing our behavior is its own kind of scary; it's not easy to say "yes" to scrutiny.

We've all encountered people who require ongoing praise. No matter how often or loudly we applaud them, they need more. They soon exhaust us. It softens our frustration toward them when we understand that their heart has a hole in it and the affirmation we and others offer tends to trickle out. Unfortunately, the lost encouragement isn't growing flowers; it's just evaporating as if it never existed, which sends them running back to us for more. In time, we find ourselves darting down grocery aisles at the store in an attempt to avoid them. We grow tired of refilling them, knowing like a flawed pot with a leak, our praise is never enough.

Honestly, we all appreciate encouragement, but when we are chasing after people-praise and it's never enough, something else is going on. If we keep bringing up a subject to gain approval and, even after being affirmed, we run around trying to hear more praise from others, we are either narcissistic or we have bought into the lie that we aren't acceptable and grasping is our way of trying to feel better about ourselves. Human ingenuity invents ways to survive, but compliment gathering is not the solution. Compliments aren't sturdy enough to hold up to a lie, and a lie is usually the cause of such self-seeking. Kudos are like armloads of flowers—lovely, but soon wilted.

What has helped me when I start fishing for compliments is to spot my needy behavior, and to do two things. First, I need to stop asking others to give me what only God can provide. Second, I defend my heart with his counsel against the lie that I lack worth; it's the only thing capable of breaking a lie that has Velcroed to my (our) spirit usually at a young age.

Human ingenuity invents ways to survive,
but compliment gathering is not the solution.
Compliments aren't sturdy enough to hold
up to a lie, and a lie is usually the cause of
such self-seeking. Kudos are like armloads
of flowers—lovely, but soon wilted.

Another vital step is to self-nurture—speaking to myself in hymns and spiritual songs, singing, and making a melody in my heart to the Lord. For years, when feeling insecure, I have sung to myself the hymns my mother sang when I was a child, while she cleaned house. The old hymns were full of strong reinforcements for a person's faith. Don't tell anyone, but my guest bathroom has at least fifty old hymns, torn from a hymnal and taped on the walls. (Please don't call the hymnal police!) I figure it's the only time some people ever sit down so I thought while they are still, they can be reminded of "What a Friend We Have in Jesus."

Speaking of songs, I find being in nature, where I can hear birds sing and breezes hum in the trees, eases my inner angst.

Sometimes I wonder if robins and mockingbirds are singing hymns. Listen closely next time and see what you think. I know they can be squawky (like us), but sometimes their sound is transcendent. I'm especially fond of the sparrows' offerings—those wee birds in house frocks trilling their hearts out atop fence post and roof peak.

I am aware of Christ's presence and pleasure as I write and paint, so when a lie rises up that I am not loved, I will paint, quite often a bird. Perhaps because they are small and yet our God provides for them and takes note when they fall. It comforts me, as does reading and penning poems.

Stillness also helps me; I can hear more clearly and am therefore more likely to identify the voice of God. It's sometimes a whisper on a butterfly's wing, in a reflective sparkle on morning dew, or in the moon crescent as it leans into the night. Sometimes it's his reassuring voice within me verifying his love.

Let me ask, how do you cooperate with God by taking care of yourself? What is it that helps you hear him? For many, it's music. Do you have songs that make your toes tap and your heart sing? What comforts you and reassures you of his love? For some, it's animals. (I have a dear friend who raises goats, horses, bees, and chickens, and when life is hard she heads to the barn. Let me just say those animals have heard an earful. They've been free therapists at times for her broken heart.)

Let me ask, how do you cooperate with God by taking care of yourself? What is it that helps you hear him? For many, it's music. Do you have songs that make your toes tap and your heart sing? What comforts you and reassures you of his love?

God knows us. He was there during the knitting together process of our very being and therefore understands what will help our spirits stay supple and well. We are all unique and respond differently. Being around a goat wouldn't work for me, but a palette full of paint somehow helps me with my stress. I have a neighbor who works diligently as a nurse, which, while rewarding, is also stressful. Her way of letting go of other people's pain and her own is to go to the stable to visit and ride her horse. She can't explain why it helps; she just knows it does, so she makes time for horse therapy. Her husband's stress level drops when he heads for a piano or his ukulele to create music. Some sew, which according to one seamstress friend, helps her stitch her faith back into place.

A pastor's wife who was also a pottery painter, told me when she could no longer paint she hoped the Lord would take her home. He did. The pottery work she did was the last way she had found to minister beauty to the lives of others. That was years ago and to this day, whenever I drink from one of her vine-covered cups, I'm reminded of what God used in her life to give her a sense of mission until he brought her home.

When our artistic results become our sense of worth, we miss the point of our value, which is not based in what we do, but whose we are. We need to understand if we could not paint one more picture, write one more poem, cook one more dinner, entertain one more weary traveler, we would still be loved.

The temptation of course is that we would put more importance on our creative efforts than on the Lord, not realizing our creativity and comfort is an expression of his care for us, a declaration of our worth. While the results of our efforts are often expressed in our gardens, sermons, journals, etc., what is truly vital is the quality of our relationship with Christ as our Savior and Lord. When our artistic results become our sense of worth, we miss the point of our value, which is not based in what we do, but whose we are. We need to understand if we could not paint one more picture, write one more poem, cook one more dinner, entertain one more weary traveler, we would still be loved.

How kind of Christ to give us a sense of purpose through our faith in him and our gifts from him. May we be mindful that our gift is not more important than the gift of his life offered at Calvary. When my friend lost her physical functions of mobility and speech because of Lou Gehrig's disease, did she lose her worth? Absolutely not. Her identity was in Christ, not in her health or her abilities. May I say she continued to powerfully influence and change lives because of the strong presence of Christ manifested in her weakness until her last breath. She faced her fears and grew stronger. She was funny, brave, and deeply spiritual throughout the ten years of her silent journey. I wouldn't have even known that was possible had I not seen it with my own eyes and talked with her caregivers who counted it a privilege to work for her. For years she could only communicate with one eyebrow that she could lift and drop and type on the commuter with one flinching muscle on the side of her knee. Her body was broken but her spirit thrived.

When we grasp our worth in Christ by believing what he says we relax our fretting, striving, and neediness. We learn that to rest in Christ is to meet him in green pastures of contentment. His love liberates us from depending on man's compliments and frees us to more fully participate in praising our God—the One who tenderly cares for us.

Deliberate on . . .

"But he said to me, 'My grace is sufficient for you, for my power is made perfect in weakness.' Therefore I will boast all the more gladly about my weaknesses, so that Christ's power may rest on me" (2 Corinthians 12:9 NIV).

Discuss . . .

- To whom do you look for approval?
- What are some of the signs of a healthy self-concept?
- When do you feel needy?

8

Basket Case

I once was lost, but now
am found, Was blind,
but now I see.

—John Newton

I mentioned Moses early on in this book and I bet you thought I forgot him. He is one of my top ten favorite Bible heroes. I love him because he started off his life as a basket case when his mom slipped him into an ark of bulrushes to protect him from the drowning of boy babies. This diabolical tactic by the Egyptians was to keep the ranks of the Israelites thinned out. However, Pharaoh's daughter found the baby in the reeds while she was bathing, took pity on the child, and brought him home to raise as her own. Moses lived a life of luxury and indulgence until he rebelled, killed a man in the heat of injustice, and ran away to save his own life.

So why am I so drawn to this rebel outlaw? Well, I too started off as a basket case, lived an indulged (spoiled) life, and was a rebel runaway. Moses had no qualifications to be a leader of God's people by their standards, nor do I, yet God called us both to serve in ways we could not imagine. Moses spent forty years tending sheep and forty years leading people. (Hmm, evidently God thought Moses' years with sheep was good preparation for dealing with stubborn, straying, vulnerable people.) I, too, am at a forty-year life marker. I have bounded about the land that long proclaiming the Lord to literally millions of people (a privilege that still makes me gasp).

When we think about it, who in their right mind would assign Moses the job of leader when he was raised by the enemy, committed a murder, and went on the lam? Unlikely choice, I must say.

When we think about it, who in their right mind would assign Moses the job of leader when he was raised by the enemy, committed a murder, and went on the lam? Unlikely choice, I must say.

And me? I never anticipated or set out to be a speaker or a writer. Why would I? I couldn't even face a new day with hope in my heart. My prayer was to get to the grocery store and home again, not to charge boldly into the market place. I'm telling you, God is into the unlikely! I was a runaway, a high school dropout, a teenage bride, and, by the time I hit my twenties, an agoraphobic. With those stats would you have chosen me as a inspirational voice for women? Nope, me either.

Years ago a woman from my community asked to meet with me, which I agreed to. I actually thought she was looking for encouragement, but instead she had come to tell me how unqualified I was to do what I was doing. I'm sure she was surprised to learn I couldn't have agreed with her more. My résumé was proof of her claim. Who can explain God and his ways? He uses whom he chooses, whether that be a basket case or an ex-agoraphobic. Broken people have never stopped God from achieving his purposes.

Here's the biggie that Moses and I share: we both felt inadequate for the tasks at hand . . . he *felt* like a basket case. It made him stammer to think about being a spokesperson. He begged God for a front man to be the voice for his people. God gave him his brother Aaron for that job, but interestingly enough, it's Moses we hear confronting Pharaoh and verbally guiding his people.

For years I would get sick before I spoke; I was certain the audience would suddenly realize how broken I was and the "gig" would be up. The truth was I couldn't have covered up my blaring weakness if I tried. Within minutes of hitting the stage I would blurt out my insecurity without even meaning to, only to have women identify and embrace me.

Do I think I'm a Moses? Heavens, no! But you can see why I was encouraged by the life of this knee-knocking leader.

I want to challenge you to find a person in Scripture you relate to and study their story. You will be surprised what you will learn about them and about yourself. The Holy Spirit is a revealer of truth and sheds light to lead and guide us. So ask him for his companionship as you study and don't resist his promptings. They are loving nudges to a fuller faith.

Don't know where to begin? Consider . . .

Joseph was rejected by his siblings and falsely sent to prison.

Abigail took brave steps to protect her people from her husband's foolish choices.

Ruth, a young widow, starting a new life in a new land.

Jonah was given a message of mercy to deliver to a people he hated.

And among my favorites are the friends who conspired to help their buddy be healed, even if that meant raising the roof.

There is no end to the life lessons packed in-between Genesis and Revelation to help us face our fears and grow stronger.

I am fascinated and inspired by courageous people, like Old Testament Deborah. Now, she was no basket case. In times when it was unheard of for women to lead, Deborah was a judge, dispensing wisdom, and then physically leading her people into battle. In fact, Barak the commander of the army refused to go to battle unless Deborah marched at his side. She agreed. Hello! *She agreed*. I would have sent a text to Barak saying, "Let me get back to you on that . . . like in a week from never."

This was no small task. We are talking ten thousand soldiers led by Deborah and Barak going up against an army that had nine hundred iron chariots for starters and a sea of soldiers. Just the sound of iron chariots tends to defeat my quivering heart. But the Lord went before his people with great storms and suddenly what appeared to be the enemies' advantage—the iron chariots—were their downfall, as they became mired and overturned. The enemy was either swept away in the ensuing floods or killed by the sword. I love the last words in that account, which say, "So the land had rest for forty years" (Judges 5:31 NKJV). God bless Deborah for doing the brave thing.

What are the life lessons? First, friend, that God may ask you to rise up and lead in ways that will take humility and courage, and Deborah has set the example. The people who you were counting on may let you down, but God is with you for the battle you face. The enemy may intimidate you with his strength, but God is able to overthrow his schemes. And ultimately, in this trying world, God is your source of rest.

We fought a hard battle at our house last year. My husband had cataract surgery that, on the third day, went amiss. Les was sitting at the table when he suddenly went blind in the eye they had operated on. Unfortunately his other eye, which had been his bad eye, had little to no vision in it. So for all intents and purposes he was blind and in terrible pain. It took many doctor visits and drugs to finally get the pain under control. Les's pain tolerance is high so when it escalated to the point he couldn't bare it, I knew it had to be excruciating. The doctors performed multiple surgeries with no results. I can't even count the number of times they had to stick needles directly into his eyeball. (Pincushion comes to mind.)

As you can imagine it didn't take long for depression to set in. Les's balance was compromised before he lost his sight from neuropathy in his legs, but after he lost his sight he had many falls leaving him bloodied, bruised, and angry. He sat for hours in our bedroom, silent, often in the dark.

I was heartsick for Les, but I knew we both couldn't be downcast. So I rose up with God's help to be a "cheergiver" as well as a caregiver. I tried to lift his spirits and keep him hopeful. I wanted to be a Deborah and dispense wisdom, but honestly it didn't look good. So I dispensed his favorite foods, which seemed like wisdom, because it brought him at least temporary entertainment, distraction, and comfort.

God may ask you to rise up and lead in ways that will take humility and courage, and Deborah has set the example. The people who you were counting on may let you down, but God is with you for the battle you face. The enemy may intimidate you with his strength, but God is able to overthrow his schemes.

I think the hardest thing for him was his inability to drive. It took away his independence, which seemed to eat at his sense of worth. I would tell him, "I've driven you crazy for years and now I get to drive you around town." He didn't laugh at my weak attempt to lighten the circumstance. And quite honestly I'm not a great driver and I have no sense of direction, which probably was at the front of his mind.

Our friend Steve Anderson would often be our driver, and he sat with us for hours on surgery day, offering us comfort with his presence. Our son Jason took his dad to endless follow-up doctor appointments. Our grandsons Justin and Noah would hang out with their papa knowing they brought him strength to press on. And there were many others who showed him kindnesses during this dark season.

Les would try to function but then he'd fall and he'd be angry at himself and disappointed all over again in the doctors. This is when the enemy would move in with iron chariots full of lies and discouragement and drive over Les's vulnerability. I could see my dear husband's spirit sink deeper into the muck of misery. Month after month after month, Les stumbled and fell and wept.

I tended to his wounds from the falls, dispensed his twenty-one eyedrops a day, wrapped and packed his eye day and night, prepared his happy meals, and beckoned him on. I was grateful I could walk at his side but sad I couldn't fix his despair.

Eight months into our battle I was standing in the living room and Les was sitting in a chair facing the fireplace when he said, "Patsy, I think I can see the light from the fireplace." After another moment passed, he looked up and said, "I see the outline of the blades on the ceiling fan." We didn't know what to think. Was he imagining it? I helped him into the bedroom and into bed. The next morning Les looked up at me with a big grin and announced, "I see your face."

The doctors are totally baffled. They can't believe Les's vision returned. They said it's just not possible. It has been five months now and to everyone's amazement his vision continues to improve. He went in and had his other eye operated on (brave man!) and that surgery was an immediate success, so Les is able to drive again. His balance has improved greatly, so we've had only one fall in months.

Oh, happy days!

Life can be scary. We need each other. I feel braver when someone is at my side, don't you? That was the plan from the beginning of time . . . that we would link arms and faith and realize that what we can't do, God can. From Moses to Deborah to family and doctors, we were meant to be cheerleaders, care-givers, and promoters of faith. Even if you feel like a basket case, are asked to do or bear more than you think you can, or find yourself marching through hardship alone, there is One who goes before you, stands beside you, and has your back.

Deliberate on . . .

"Bear one another's burdens, and thereby fulfill the law of Christ" (Galatians 6:2 NASB).

Discuss . . .

- When is the last time you had to ask someone for help?
- Why do you think it's so hard to be vulnerable?
- Think of someone in Scripture that you identify with. What do you have in common?

9

Spring Thaw

It is spring again. The earth
is like a child that knows
poems by heart.

—Rainer M. Rilke

B eing (or becoming!) sane in this crazy world takes intentionality. Especially on those days we feel like a basket case. We are called to make purposeful choices, in faith, as we grasp our identity in Christ. We have hope for today, hope for tomorrow, and a destiny of hope.

But I don't have to tell you that hard things, scary things, and even weird things are happening daily in this topsy-turvy society we call our life. So what can we do about that?

I believe we have to do what we can to be sanity contributors. This means we make up our minds to be mentally fit—fit for mature reasoning. If I had a banner I could hold up for the world to see, it would read, "Think Smart . . . Do Your Part."

So what is our part? It depends on where we are.

If we are trapped in our home because we are afraid (as I was), then our part is to work tenaciously to get well. We begin facing our fears . . . not because it's easy, but because we have made up our mind to grow healthy. This means we inch our way out our front door, greet our neighbors at the mailbox, and learn to function once again in society. We learn to move our muscles to obey our will. As we begin to function, our personal dignity is gradually restored. You see, the world needs us to be an example so they know that they, too, can make their way through scary times and survive. We can, by virtue of new liberties in our lives, become an example of hope to the rest of the world.

Recovery is costly because it requires us to function in our weakness, and we live in a society that promotes super heroes making us feel "less-than" in comparison. As we take difficult but deliberate baby steps, gradually a spark of hope ignites within us, which is all it takes to start a flame. Heaven knows, the world needs lamplighters.

If we are someone who is depressed we need to reach out for help, take our meds, and deliberately step into the light. Society is looking for light-bearers who know what it means to risk—risk taking the next shaky step toward recovery. Recovery is costly because it requires us to function in our weakness, and we live in a society that promotes super heroes making us feel "less-than" in comparison. As we take difficult but deliberate baby steps, gradually a spark of hope ignites within us, which is all it takes to start a flame. Heaven knows, the world needs lamplighters.

If we are deeply insecure, our part is to realize that hiding in our weakness only adds to our angst (at least it did mine). I want you to grow strong in your sense of divine destiny because I found in doing so it called "brave" out of me. I want you to practice affirmations that agree with God's Word because I found they combat the disabling lies of the enemy.

Find others who will walk hand in hand with you as you take your shaky steps; when I faced my darkest challenges, my praying friends helped hold my arms up as I took my next steps. I also found that when I was willing to assist someone else it took my focus off my dilemma, which helped to reinvigorate my determination, while it encouraged someone else toward their own recovery. We were meant to be in community, so we fulfill our calling.

It is my hope and prayer that our lives show others what it means to stand tall in our Christ-filled identity. The world needs voices of courage, and your voice, blended with all of ours, is necessary.

God knows our lives take on added purpose when we feel we have done something that has contributed to another life, so he invites us to be involved with his intentions, which are always, always good.

It's true isn't it? When I go back over journal ramblings I've scribbled through the years, I find they are always ones I wrote during times of depression, times of loss, times of confusion, times of . . . well, you get the idea. Hardships cause us to reach out and "up" in desperation, which in turn, helps us risk change. And hardships are usually the incentive to change.

During one dark season of burnout, when I worked far too long without rest, I wrote this poem, entitled "Winter":

Winter came early and would not depart,

Winter came early to a tender, young heart.

Frozen inside, the child would not feel,

Locked in her pain, she could not heal.

Icy responses replaced her trust;

Numbed by life's season,

Her soul formed a crust.

Hardened by bitterness,

Chilled with despair,

Encased in the cold with no one to care.

Icicle tears clung to her face,

Frigid reminders of her shame and disgrace.

Winter came early to a tender young heart,

Winter came early and would not depart.

Wow . . . I didn't know that was in me. I have learned exhaustion sometimes opens up old wounds, some even from our youth, which we may not even realize we carry. For me, when my strength was at an all-time low, it was as if my vulnerability opened a cellar door to my heart and these words escaped. I didn't know this much sadness was crouching in the shadows of my memories. We seldom do.

Once I wrote this poem, I took it to my counselor who was assisting me through the burnout recovery. She heard the pain in each line and offered me words of insight, and a type of comfort that was tender but not indulgent. Then she said something I'll never forget: "I look forward to the next poem, the one of redemption."

Throughout the weeks and months of my recovery, I thought of her comment many times and then one day, when it was time and I was rested, I wrote "Spring":

Spring came late, late in her years,
Spring came late to thaw her tears.
The little glazed sculpture
Stood frozen in place,
Till the light of the Son
dissolved her disgrace.

The icicles fell to the ground below:

her heart, warmed with love, melted the snow.

No longer a statue in an ice-cold rhyme,

No longer a victim locked in a crime.

Spring came late to thaw her tears,

Spring came late, late in her years.

Now, I chuckle to myself that I called my forties "late in my years," but compared to childhood it did seem like it then. Now my forties seem more like my youth!

As I look back on that burnout season I realize I felt as though no one heard me when I kept saying, "I am so tired. I can't keep up this pace. I need time off." I was functioning like the child in the rhyme; I thought I didn't have a choice, and I was waiting for someone to rescue me, instead of doing the adult work of taking care of myself.

One season of exhaustion connected to a childhood season of loneliness and words set off by pain gave way to venting carefully hidden secrets. I first vented through the poem and then to my counselor who helped my heart open a little wider. I became more compassionate and less vindictive toward others and myself. And I became saner and braver.

It was a time to "Think Smart—and Do My Part."

No one could do my recovery or reflective work for me. My journey helped me to have more than just an opinion to offer others who were suffering because now my answers rang true with experience. I began noticing that when I was in a circle of people, I could sense who was in trouble emotionally because my willingness to face truth and take responsibility for myself heightened my discernment of others.

Recently I was with someone whose behavior indicated that he was carrying bundles of pain. It came out in his nervous habits, in his defensive nature, and in his relationships. He stayed too busy, he chatted endlessly, he smoked nonstop, and he had major sleep issues. He greeted you with his list of achievements, which was never enough to satisfy his tattered soul. He never inquired about anyone else's success, afraid, I think, that it would diminish his own fragile worth. Even after several failed marriages and lost employment he was unwilling to examine his own splintered behavior.

I understand his defiance . . . his insecurity . . . his reluctance. I've been there. I've found if we don't confront our issues we will live in fear of even the hurts of others, lest their pain tip our own bucket. It made me sad for him because he was putting forth the image that he "had his act together" when nothing could have been further from the truth, and it was obvious to those who spent time with him. Facing fear helps us grow stronger.

Of course, it's scary to think if we own our story we'll have to face our failures and embrace stored pain. I mean, who purposes to be sad or mad or scared? And while it's accurate that the road to a recovering heart is jagged, it's also true that when we own our inconsistencies and feel yesterday's pain, that makes space for healing, true humility, and charitable grace. Oh, what blessed relief!

There are steps that can help us to handle our turmoil. To begin, we have to be willing to dig deep and take stock of what's going on in our lives. How would you answer the following statements about yourself?

- Do you consistently feel lonely even in a crowd of known people?
- Are your feelings easily hurt?
- Are you holding grudges? (Are there people you would never invite over from your family, church, work, and neighborhood? Why?)

- Do you overreact regularly? (Would the people around you agree with your answer?)
- Are you addicted to pleasing people?
- Do you use anger to control the people in your zip code?
- Do you have physical aggravations that suggest your stress levels are a tad high? (e.g., hives, ulcers, fever blisters, low energy, grinding teeth, nail biting, etc.)
- Does guilt and/or shame whittle away at your worth?
- Are you moody, sulky, or manipulative? Do you use silence to punish people? Do you withhold love to get your way?
- Do you sleep too much? Do you struggle with insomnia?
- Do you eat too much or too often? Do you starve yourself?

I have my hand raised because at one time or another, multiples of these described my behavior. My body and mind's imbalance was alerting me to my issues, but I wasn't listening until my symptoms were so paralyzing I could no longer deny that I was in trouble and needed help—not help to fix my husband, not help to change my kids, not help to adjust my friends, but help to work on me.

If answering "yes" to any of the above questions troubles you or you feel stuck, my hat's off to you because that is the first step toward change: *ownership*.

But there's a second step, which is *educating yourself* on recovery strategies. When I was struggling, I took the next step and went to my family doctor, took medications, and went to a group for people with anxiety (at the time, I didn't even know there were others who were struggling with issues like mine). God used all of those choices to help me on the path to recovery.

And the third step is *integrating truth* into your inward parts. I am so grateful God meets us in our darkest hours. He has given us his Word to be a lamp to shine light on our path. But he doesn't want us to stand still on our path. He asks us to meet him by moving forward in faith—even if it's just taking a baby step. Sometimes taking initiative requires hard work, time, and counsel of others who have walked the path and are a few steps ahead of us.

Quite honestly, we are all broken because we live in a fallen world.

So is "thinking smart" enough to maintain our sanity? Sadly, not always. Some things are outside of our control and require intervention.

It was heartbreaking to learn that the beloved actor/comedian Robin Williams committed suicide. When it was announced, social media lit up with bewilderment and grief. We as a society are sad to lose a man who helped us laugh and cry—two ways God wove into our design to help us cope.

Laughter has a multitude of meanings. There are times we laugh until we splash tears of untouched grief. And then we weep until sorrows soften and we can laugh again.

Our response to those who help bring us emotional relief is one of gratitude. What Robin did for his audiences brought great relief and for that we will always be grateful. But beyond his obvious gifts, we are now aware of the tragedy of someone despairing to the point of ending his life. Somewhere deep within, I think some of us wonder if we are in danger of doing the same thing.

Robin was a complicated man full of contradictions that came out in his unstable behavior. He had a brilliant mind but, by his own admission, he was a troubled soul. Robin admitted he was afraid, lonely, and sad. He used his pain to brilliantly perform roles that were tender and sometimes bizarre.

No one fully understands the depth of sadness or despair in another soul, nor what one can bear, except Christ. I believe our wounded Shepherd weeps over, and with, the anguished and tormented. He promises he is near to the brokenhearted (read Psalm 34:18).

I don't believe most suicide victims are in touch with the great grief they leave for others to wade through, because they often believe they are more of a burden to their loved ones than a blessing, and that the weight of their disability and/or shame is too great to continue to bear.

There is help . . . *there is hope.*

Some of us are more delicately woven together than others. That can be a hardship, but on the underside of delicate there is often brilliance and creativity. Do not rob yourself or others of what you have to offer. Don't give up.

Please don't hurt yourself. *You matter.*

There are medications, therapy, behavior modification groups, and other services that help people make it through the bleakest of times. If you have moods that don't lift, if you have thoughts of harming yourself, if you aren't eating, or find yourself withdrawing, even from those you love, please reach out. Tell someone you need help. Call a suicide hotline and talk. Sometimes airing your sadness will help you enough so that you can find some relief. Make an appointment with your medical doctor to make sure you haven't had a hormonal crash, or a chemical imbalance, or that your thyroid hasn't gone bonkers, or one of a myriad of other things that make us feel like we are coming unglued. If you detect these symptoms in someone you love, take them seriously, come alongside them, and help them find resources.

The journey back to feeling "normal," "acceptable," or "loved" may take time, but it will be worth working toward and waiting for. None of us is beyond needing help. So we mustn't build walls that shut others out. We were designed to be interactive, as difficult as that can be at times. Even though we often cause each other pain, we also bring each other hope through our own survival. We need each other's support and stories.

The journey back to feeling "normal," "acceptable," or "loved" may take time, but it will be worth working toward and waiting for. None of us is beyond needing help. So we mustn't build walls that shut others out. We were designed to be interactive, as difficult as that can be at times.

God is not asking us to bear the weight of the world. He's got that covered, but he is asking us to run our race with grace as he measures it out. And here's the incentive: He will be with us.

Remember, there is good news.

Winter won't last forever. Spring is coming.

Deliberate on . . .

> "I waited patiently for the L
ORD;
>
> And He inclined to me and heard my cry.
>
> He brought me up out of the pit of destruction, out of
> the miry clay,
>
> And He set my feet upon a rock making my footsteps
> firm.
>
> He put a new song in my mouth, a song of praise to
> our God;
>
> Many will see and fear
>
> And will trust in the L
ORD" (Psalm 40:1–3 NASB).

Discuss . . .

- Have you tried to put your sad feelings into words or a poem?
- What about your joyful feelings? Think about a happy day—a wedding, a child's birth, a Christmas—and write a paragraph or a page.
- Do you relate with the word *unglued*? When did you feel that way? Why?

10

Welcome Home, Joy

A greater joy is preceded by

a greater suffering.

—Charles Spurgeon

For me, because my good feelings had been shut down for so long, it took time before I could feel or even identify positive emotions. The journey toward healthy responses seemed impossible at first. Sadness had been my habitat, so it was a huge adjustment for me—as if I had stepped out of a dark cave and was blinded by sunlight and uncertain of my footing. I had bare-handed my way around in the dank air of fear for what seemed like ages, and it had become familiar and strangely protective. I had made the cold walls of despair my touch-point.

When happy feelings came back into my life, even a trickle of cheerfulness was overwhelming. I wasn't certain what to do with it, but I quickly became desperate not to lose it. I tried to pump up the good feelings until they came like circus balloons, but the pressure stretched them past their intentions and they would burst. It took me higher than was healthy for me, leaving me heady and dizzy, only to then drop me lower than I had been before I had stuck my head out of the cave.

Feeling good didn't feel safe.

I had to learn to sit with joy and become friends again . . . to feel its sweet embrace and to delight in its presence without allowing myself the temporary luxury of giddiness in my attempt to make it more than it was intended to be. I reminded myself that this lovely feeling was not meant to be exploited to escape my sadness, but was intended to be medicinal to heal the ruptures within me, and to remind me at a deeper level that I was loved. Just because, at times, it came and left, that did not signal abandonment or failure on my part, and it didn't mean I wouldn't experience good feelings again.

It often would take me days and sometimes weeks to figure out if I had enjoyed myself with friends or family. That's how "out of touch" with myself I was. I seemed to be on a delayed timer. I know that sounds odd, but I was a suppressed soul.

For instance, we would have a holiday gathering and afterwards someone would ask, "How was it? Did you have a good time?" I would nod my head to be polite and smile at the asker, but I wouldn't truly know for weeks. Gradually, I would think of a conversation I had that day or a compliment I received, or laughter that we shared, and with it would come a wisp of a feeling, maybe tenderness or pleasure, and I would think, *Oh, that was a fun time!*

If you are emotionally shut down or delayed, please know the registry of our feelings is important to help us connect with ourselves, with others, and with God. The popular phrase "be current" or "be in the moment" is good counsel. Learning the names of our feelings is also important so we know where we are; they help us to pinpoint our existence. Often I can remember saying I was angry only to discover later that I was afraid. Or vice versa; I would think I was afraid when I was sitting on a hot bed of coals.

Please know the registry of our feelings is important to help us connect with ourselves, with others, and with God. The popular phrase "be current" or "be in the moment" is good counsel. Learning the names of our feelings is also important so we know where we are; they help us to pinpoint our existence.

I don't know how you were raised, but in my family you could express words and actions of fear, but anger was not acceptable. That needed to be stifled. Anger was considered a rude expression rather than an appropriate emotion for having been violated. So throughout my life I often covered my anger up, put a lid on it, until one day I couldn't anymore. Then I became a temper-driven young woman willing to do battle at the drop of a hat, and actually part of that came from my fear. I felt like a Patsy-in-a-Box . . . wind me up and it was anybody's guess who would pop out.

We are intricate people.

I'm relieved that I don't have to untangle the ball of emotional twine within me by myself. That's why we have . . .

- Jesus, our gentle Shepherd;
- the guidance and comfort of the Holy Spirit;
- the counsel of God's Word;
- and each other.

Here's another truth: I don't have to untangle it all at once. Just deal with what I know in the moment, according to truth . . . one day at a time.

Knotted twine life's twisted pain,
words unspoken, acid rain.
Tears forgotten, loss, despair,
buried joy, languish there.
Risk the journey, voice the fear,
loose the grief, feel Yahweh near.

Oh, Gentle Shepherd, quiet, blessed,

be my safety, be my rest.

Here's a question I had to ask myself: Do I have a responsibility in the recovery of joy? Isn't joy God's job? Don't we wait around hoping he will dump a bucket of joy over us? Or feelings of peace, hope, love, etc.?

I used to think it was all up to God, but now I believe that we are invited by our heavenly Father to join in our own recovery by our choices. God invites us to create an inner atmosphere conducive to good feelings like joy and gratitude when he instructs us to "rejoice and again I say rejoice," "be anxious for nothing," and "in all things give thanks." God tells us that to give thanks is his will. He knew if we would purposefully express gratitude, that we would be more aware of his joy-filled presence in the midst of our identity, our calamity, and our destiny.

During my years of depression God didn't knock on my door and announce joy, hope, love, peace, etc., were coming to my house today. It wasn't until I agreed to let go of my deep melancholy, a little at a time, and open my heart to the possibility of God at work within me that nurturing emotions rose up to a feeling level.

So how do we let go of melancholy—especially when it feels Velcroed to our souls? I can tell you how I tripped my way along, but I am not suggesting this is the only way toward wellness, nor am I saying that the wobbly path I took is right for you in sequence. God is optionally diverse, but beginning somewhere is the first important step.

I used to think it was all up to God, but now I believe that we are invited by our heavenly Father to join in our own recovery by our choices. God invites us to create an inner atmosphere conducive to good feelings like joy and gratitude when he instructs us to "rejoice and again I say rejoice," "be anxious for nothing," and "in all things give thanks."

I entertained so much negativity that it took an hourly, if not moment-by-moment, scrutiny of my thoughts to catch the bad cycles, like self-loathing. I had to practice "kind" self-talk. That wasn't an easy transition for someone like me who had beat myself up for years. At first I didn't believe what I was saying; that I had value, that I could recover, that I had something of worth to offer others, etc. Therefore, I had to speak truth into myself *by faith* since the lies I had embraced were certainly not serving me well. When I say "by faith" I don't mean to suggest I had a strong spiritual center at that time, but I felt like I was out of options and "by faith" was my last ditch shaky attempt to survive. What I learned "by faith" is that our center grows stronger when we feed it nutritional offerings.

I began to read the Bible with a passion. When I came across verses that caught my interest, I would sit with them. I remember meditating for months on Romans 12:2: "And do not be conformed to this world, but be transformed by the renewing of your mind, so that you may prove what the will of God is, that which is good and acceptable and perfect" (NASB). That verse is so packed with counsel I'm not sure it can be totally unpacked, but it has been a guiding light on my path. I resource it often. When verses grab my attention I write them down. Read them aloud. Memorize them. Ask the Lord to counsel me with them. Some verses were obvious as to what I needed to do and what they meant; others not so much.

If you are new to reading the Bible may I encourage you to start with Genesis. The first chapter alone is worth your time and pondering. You might want to journal as you read because I found the stories stirred up insight and questions, and your journal is a place to keep track of those. Don't worry or give up if you don't understand parts of it; even scholars are still puzzling over portions. Ask yourself where you need hope. It could be your relationships or the rearing of children or your finances; ask God to open your understanding as you read.

Since fear was my most coddled emotion, I searched for verses about it. I used a concordance at the back of my Bible to guide me to the verses and often found myself in Psalms and Proverbs where I ended up spending a good deal of time. I also read and reread the Gospel of John and the book of Philippians.

Music helped me heal but I had to be selective because some songs brought back bundles of sad memories, which my sensitive heart could not afford. I also read every book I could get my hands on about practical Christianity, including *Disciples Are Made Not Born, The Christian's Secret of a Happy Life,* and *Hinds Feet on High Places.* Such are not wave-a-magic-wand books but gutsy instruction about our journey with its hardships and joy. For years I have read daily devotions by Oswald Chambers and Charles Spurgeon.

From my beloved volume of *Morning and Evening,* Spurgeon wrote, "May your character not be a writing upon the sand, but an inscription upon the rock."

That's my longing today for me and my prayer for you: that we would stay close to our Companion, Shepherd, and Teacher, Jesus, all the way home. For therein lies safety for your heart and your developing character. Not that your journey might not be treacherous at times, and feel isolating, but that with your steadfast, rock-solid Savior, you would not travel alone or without resources.

Deliberate on . . .

"Weeping may endure for a night,

But joy comes in the morning" (Psalm 30:5b NKJV).

Discuss . . .

- Write down a time where and when you felt God's presence in a crisis you faced. When you remind yourself it helps to assure you of his ongoing interest and involvement with the things that matter to you.

- Do you believe God uses your deepest pain for holy purposes? Explain why you believe the way you do.

11

Sizzle

*I want a life that sizzles and
pops and makes me laugh
out loud.*

—Shauna Niequist

Fear convinced me that I was undeserving of laughter and that the best I could hope for was a constricted life where I was bullied around by shame. Because of those years of wrestling with my insecurities, I didn't know that I could have a life with sizzle and pop. I read where Jesus had come to give life and that more abundant, but I had learned to believe it didn't apply to me.

The journey through my fears and into truth has not been quick or easy, but it has been redemptive. From hiding away frightened in my bedroom to speaking before literally millions of women about liberty, it is far beyond what I could have dreamed for myself. Along the way, Jesus has confirmed within me that we all are more than we know because he, the Lord, is greater than we can imagine. He is infinity. Can you imagine timelessness? Me either. That is why we will never finish searching out the love of God. I am convinced only he could and would rescue a woman as broken and splintered as I was, and some days still can be, and position me to minister to others. Only God.

Life can be intimidating, but here's the bottom line: Jesus is still on the throne. His promise for peace in the midst of storms holds true. His overflowing joy is continually offered. His hope is unending. And heaven remains the destiny for those who love the Lord.

So can we add sizzle and pop to our existence?

I say a resounding *yes!* I bet you'll join me after you read the following three steps that helped me to participate in a fuller life. This is your invitation to begin and/or renew your commitment to gratitude, generosity, and graciousness.

Join me in practicing *gratitude*. Stats are out from hospitals, counselors, and doctors that claim the quality of our heart-life is deeper and wider when we are grateful. It keeps us from being self-consumed and melancholy, which is healthy for our mind. A thriving minds help us maintain better physical and emotional well-being.

When our son was in a coma for twenty-one days, you can imagine how we as his parents anguished. Every day the team of doctors could offer no hope for his recovery. While we were waiting on God's final say-so, several things happened that helped us survive the daily tension of our circumstances.

In 1 Thessalonians 5:18, we are encouraged to "in everything give thanks; for this is God's will for you in Christ Jesus" (NASB). Notice it says "in everything" we are to give thanks, not "for everything." It would be cruel for God to instruct us to be glad our son was suffering and near death, but instead he asks us to find reasons to be grateful during our hardship. God knows gratitude will help us to face our fears and grow inwardly stronger.

I remember a moment when our tension was palpable and I felt like Les and I were about to implode so I said, "Let's take a walk." We went to the seating area at the end of the hall; no one else was there, and we sat in silence. We seemed to be out of words to comfort each other . . . and that's when it happened. We heard someone . . . singing. A voice as pure and clear as any I had ever heard wafted across the waiting room. We had no idea where it was coming from as we looked around and then back at each other, puzzled. I got up and began following the sound and behind a half wall that led to the women's restroom, down on her hands and knees scrubbing the wall tiles, was a cleaning lady singing her heart out, totally unaware of our presence, our story, or our need.

The song? "He Keeps Me Singing."

There's within my heart a melody
Jesus whispers sweet and low,
"Fear not, I am with thee, peace, be still,
In all of life's ebb and flow."

Jesus, Jesus, Jesus,

Sweetest Name I know,

Fills my every longing,

Keeps me singing as I go.

Our soloist did not see me nor did I speak to her. Instead, I sat back down and my husband and I allowed the ministry of the cleaning lady's overflowing heart to quiet our mounting angst. Afterwards we walked back to take up our vigil in our son's room, grateful for a gal we did not know and who had no idea what she had done for us.

The song she sang was one my mother sang when I was growing up. Mom was a woman of prayer and faith. It was so comforting to hear the words in these tumultuous moments. Somehow we felt less afraid and stronger for the journey ahead. I carried the words of that song in my conscious thoughts even after our son woke up and amazed the doctors, earning him the title of "The Miracle."

Try this today: Look for what's right in life and people, instead of what's wrong. Anybody can find the wrong, but it takes the astute to discern the right, the good, and the worthy. Then verbalize your appreciation; it adds joy-sparks to your conversations and your relationships. Words like "I appreciate you."

"You have no idea how special you are to me." "Thank you for your many kindnesses." We know these statements can change a person's day, but if you're like me, you need to be reminded. I only wish I could go back and tell that singing angel at the hospital thank you for living her faith even on her knees doing humble tasks. Sure says a lot about her. Often times we can be so caught up in our own drama we forget to say what's inside of us. Every time I speak or write about her I secretly hope she'll hear or read it and know it was her gratitude and faithfulness God used. Let's not be in such a hurry to check off the next thing on our to-do lists that we overlook important opportunities to express our gratitude.

Look for what's right in life and people, instead of what's wrong. Anybody can find the wrong, but it takes the astute to discern the right, the good, and the worthy. Then verbalize your appreciation; it adds joy-sparks to your conversations and your relationships.

Join me in growing *generousness*. I don't know about you, but I have more stuff than I need. I counted the other day and

I found twelve tubes of lipstick in drawers, pockets, and purses. What's that about? I know no one wants my used lipstick, but I bet I could find someone who would like one of my four popcorn machines. (Not sure how that happened. But I know *exactly* how I ended up with a dozen pairs of shoes under my bed, not counting the ones in the closet.) I sound like I'm trying out to be a contestant for hoarders anonymous, but I bet if you ferreted around in your cupboards and closets, not to mention your attic or garage, you too would find "extras" of something lurking about. I gave a young housewife a flock of extra wooden spoons last week that had been nesting in dust webs in my utensil drawer. She was thrilled and I was relieved to find them a good home, one where they are actually used. Then for good measure I tossed in a couple of cookbooks from my, let's just say, "chubby" collection.

When we give to others, we like ourselves better. It's that simple. Mental illness is often hallmarked by stacks of stuff . . . let's purpose not to go there. We also soon discover that less "debris" lightens our emotional load, makes maintaining our homes easier, and, best of all, I believe, it pleases the Lord, who made it his lifestyle to travel light and ask for little. So what can you give up? To whom? I think I'll start with my bulging book cabinet and then tiptoe my way to the shoes.

Generosity is not just about stuff. Sometimes for me my most treasured thing I can offer someone is time. Maybe because I'm entering into my seventieth year of life, I am aware my stint on earth is about to become my life in glory and I need to be purposed in my remaining hours (years). But I don't want what time I have left to feel like a frantic scurry where others are aware I'm in an internal gallop to get on with the next thing. I want to be present and at peace when I am with others, not distracted and flustered.

Join me in exercising *graciousness*. My name, "Patsy," means "gracious," which has been a lifelong challenge for me to grow into. Gracious for me speaks of softness and I am naturally wiry. When anyone says to me, "You are so gracious," I know God is at work.

When I think of ways to exercise graciousness inviting people into my home immediately comes to mind. Talk about necessary fun, this is it! But it didn't start as fun for me because I would get so nervous and afraid that I would be judged for not having things perfect. It took being willing to feel vulnerable before I overcame my perfectionistic roadblocks, which I had constructed. No one else but me was demanding the unattainable. I think I was afraid if people came into my home the close proximity to my life would expose just how broken I was. One thing I've learned for sure: We won't overcome our fears or grow stronger if we don't deliberately face them.

Years ago my friend MaryAnn, who was a gracious hostess, counseled me to lower my performance expectations. She said one of the sweetest memories she had was when a young couple invited her and her husband over to their modest attic apartment for hot cocoa and popcorn. That story really helped me, because I tried so hard to make things just so-so that I would wring all the fun out of the occasion. Not just for me but for my guests as well, because tension is palpable.

A few years ago during the holidays, my friend Carol was having an open house but was unable to get her bedroom renovation complete. Quite honestly, it was a construction mess; hanging mismatched wallpaper, rusty fixtures, and a scruffy sub-floor. I couldn't imagine how folks would respond to this visual eye-sore. But Carol, an artist, set up, in the middle of the room, a rickety ladder, an empty can of paint, an old paint brush, a ribbon across the open door entry, and a hand-printed sign leaning against the ladder that read, "Coming Soon . . ." It was a hit. Did Carol lose status with her guests? Far from it; she instead was applauded for her creativity and her graciousness.

Her sign also gave permission to others not to let little things prevent hospitality. Besides, now they all wanted to be invited back to see the finished work.

While it can take some planning and effort, there is nothing healthier for us than inviting in a circle of friends. We were meant to do life together. What an opportunity to make people feel comfortable, important, and included. I cherish building history with kindred friends in a warm environment. Every home we have lived in, I always pray that people will feel received and safe because I believe those are two important needs of the human soul. I know things have gone well when my guests say, "I just want to stay here. Can I move in?" Isn't that dear? I love offering folks a haven from life's hardships.

Maybe you are reluctant to swing open your doors because you are not a great cook. Do you see that raised hand? It's mine. Beyond a few dishes I am much better as a greeter, so I invite good cooks over and they either bring a dish or prepare something yummy in my kitchen. Otherwise, we order in and everyone celebrates the ease and each other. Your guests would much rather have you being present to enjoy the time than trying to be perfect, adding stress and strain.

Remember that Pinterest can serve as inspiration—it has for me! Just be careful that it doesn't feed perfectionism, which is an animal with a voracious appetite that will eat your lunch. Simplify your methods and you'll be far more likely to sizzle and pop as a gracious hostess.

While it can take some planning and effort, there is nothing healthier for us than inviting in a circle of friends. We were meant to do life together. What an opportunity to make people feel comfortable, important, and included. I cherish building history with kindred friends in a warm environment.

Today I delight in making my home tidy (not perfect), inviting (by being emotionally present), and provisional (thinking through needs ahead of time). I make sure bathrooms are friendly, seating at the table is ample, and back-up instant offerings are available in case someone has an eager appetite that night, or they show up with their unexpected guests, or someone (me) drops a tray of food. And I make sure I have my sense of humor intact.

A couple of years ago a group of our friends poured into our house ready to eat and enjoy each other's company. Included in this circle was our friend, comedian Ken Davis, who, after dinner as we were sitting in the living room, was regaling us with a very funny story. Suddenly in the middle of the story with all eyes glued on him, Ken inserted an unexpected comment that took a moment for our group to process. He said, "Oh, you have a mouse." His wife and I assured him that this was not a funny addition to his story since we both get "crazy" at even the thought of one. "No, really," he said, pointing, "there it is."

His wife, Diane, looked, then nodded; her eyes had grown unusually wide. At the same moment, she and I leapt to our feet and headed to the highest point we could access, the dining room chairs, and screeched like little girls. The mouse headed for the fireplace. The other women, being a tad saner, backed away from the fireplace into the entry. The men headed toward the invader, armed with fireplace pokers, only to discover a small opening in the old ash box at the back of the fireplace that led outside . . . and the critter had exited the building.

Had I had presence of mind, I might have been embarrassed about the mouse and felt responsible, but trust me . . . I was too concerned with my future and suggested to my husband, who was bent-over laughing, that we sell our house and move.

All that to say that some things can't be anticipated. What a chance for us to exercise *gratitude* (it could have been a python!), *generosity* (if we catch him, you can take him home), and *graciousness* (no problem folks we can handle this . . . sort of).

Gratitude.

Generosity.

Graciousness.

Yes, we can do this. And I guarantee if you do join me and embrace these three character habits, you won't be able to keep from laughing out loud. I have found investing yourself wisely comes with the benefit of joy. Even though they may seem too simple to help you combat fear, trust me—these activities pull us out of ourselves, which is a great vacation from over-thinking our life or becoming self-absorbed. Add to that the understanding that every time we face fear we grow stronger. If that's not enough, gratitude, generosity, and graciousness open us up to discovering that we truly are more, because *he is*!

Deliberate on . . .

"You will keep him in perfect peace, Whose mind is stayed on You" (Isaiah 26:3a NKJV).

Discuss . . .

- List fifteen things for which you are grateful.
- When was your last generous action or offering?
- Who is the most gracious person you know? Why is that?

CONCLUSION

Rowdy

*Never is a woman so
fulfilled as when she
chooses to underwhelm her
schedule so she can let God
overwhelm her soul.*

—Lysa TerKeurst

can't tell you how many times I've jumped in bed still rattled from a harried day and then wondered why, with my level of exhaustion, I can't sleep. By nature I'm such a rowdy girl, my family thinks I'm tightly wound. I believe them. So it's no surprise that I have to work to have a peaceful and quiet existence . . . at least before bedtime. I do know that by evening our minds are often on overdrive trying to process our day, and when we deliberately slow our pace and speak peace to ourselves it helps our minds get that work done. The result usually is then when we crawl into bed, rest follows. But I forget.

Life is harsh without any assistance from me, so when I aim to soften the edges to the degree I can, it makes a difference. I find I need to avoid tension-wracked television shows that leave me full of jangled nerves and nightmares. I have learned that the last two hours before bedtime I should be settling down my mind and emotions to recover from the day and to prepare myself for a better quality sleep. This isn't always possible, but most nights it is.

I sometimes—okay, okay . . . often—give in to the temptation to play Words with Friends and breeze through Pinterest, update my Instagram, and even send a Tweet or ten. But I've noticed that kind of concentrated activity breeds rapid eye movement, which truly isn't conducive to rest.

Many folks like to journal at night. I prefer to do that kind of work in the morning so if I stir up anything emotional inside of me I have the daylight hours to process it. I love to read in the last hours before sleep or to be read to by an audible book. My evening reading is much different than my day reading. At night I find it helps me if I settle in with a gentle novel, beautiful poems, prayers, art books, or meditative Psalms. It just makes sense, if we want to rest well in the night, we need to prepare wisely.

Sleep is important to our body's need to recover strength and to heal; it helps recharge our circulation, it improves our mood, it gives us renewed impetus to carry on, it's kind to our heart, and it even improves our looks and attitudes. My favorite result from good sleep habits is it helps my brain to think in a more reasonable way.

The topic of closing a day, and sleep, seemed like the right place to end this book, since our Shepherd calls us to quiet resting places and still waters for reasons that benefit and protect our mental health, our emotions, and our faith. I just want to say, all of us are fragile, just in somewhat different ways. And while we are different one person to the next, we are the same in that we all need love, nurturing, and a sense of our value. I found in my recovery from agoraphobia that I needed to look past my own neediness long enough to help someone else. When I did, I began to see how God wanted to use my messy story. For forty years now, he's given me this undeserved honor to speak his name to weary journeyers in need of hope. He wants to use your story as well . . . and probably already has.

Maybe I should have named this book *Reasonable* since it has been my quest. I'd like to give up more of my rowdy rabbit race for his peaceful pace. My mind left unchecked can scamper, scatter, and skip about getting into rabbit holes it does not belong in. I can actually talk my head into depression via anger and self-pity. On the other hand, I can challenge, comfort, and create in my mind reasons to stay present, active, and alert in this wonderful journey called life.

God created us with potential beyond our understanding. When we are eager to learn and are willing to make the reasonable choices even in unreasonable circumstances, we enter into the "more," and then life becomes a joy, people become necessary, and faith a privilege. Sanity is outside our grasp without an anchor and a reason to go on. That's why hope is so important to our psyche . . . the hope we find in a personal relationship with Christ.

God created us with potential beyond our understanding. When we are eager to learn and are willing to make the reasonable choices even in unreasonable circumstances, we enter into the "more," and then life becomes a joy, people become necessary, and faith a privilege.

At this juncture of my life I'm not convinced normal is an attainable or even desirable goal, but embracing our God-given uniqueness is. In fact, it's an adventure that leads us to embracing that we are more than we know because the Lord is greater— *far greater*—than we can ever imagine.

The Lord Will Be Your Confidence

"Keep sound wisdom and discretion;
So they will be life to your soul
And grace to your neck.
Then you will walk safely in your way,
And your foot will not stumble.
When you lie down, you will not be afraid;
Yes, you will lie down and your sleep will be sweet.
Do not be afraid of sudden terror,
Nor of trouble from the wicked when it comes;
For the LORD will be your confidence,
And will keep your foot from being caught."

(Proverbs 3:21b-26 NKJV)

Soothe Yourself

In a Moment of Panic . . .

1. Breathe Deep . . . release slowly
2. Relax Muscles—during exhales
3. Change Thoughts—you are not in danger—unguarded thoughts fuel anxiety
4. Remind Yourself: This Will Pass—speak to yourself kindly
5. Breathe Deep . . . release slowly
6. Relax Muscles
7. Don't Buy Into Lies—this isn't the worst spell ever, you will not die, you will not lose your mind, you are not crazy, you are not the only one
8. The More You Relax Your Muscles the Shorter Your Emotional Spin Will Be
9. Sing/Hum Music that Soothes You . . . I hum old hymns my mom sang when I was young . . . and think on the words
10. Repeat Starting with Step One

Acknowledgments

I would like to stand up and applaud Jeana Ledbetter and Kyle Olund for their involvement in this project. You, Jeana, coaxed me into revisiting my emotional years of anguish, which sounds unkind but in truth was an ongoing safeguard for my own soul. So often we can put so much distance between us and what we went through that we can become indifferent. Writing my pain of those years reminded me afresh of God's redemptive power and His many kindnesses to me. Your confident spirit and joyful heart made you both convincing and a sweetheart to work with.

Kyle, I enjoyed your get-the-job-done work style. I was encouraged by your side notes of appreciation. Thank you— it helped me to keep on the task at hand. You made what could have been tedious, timely, by your expertise and expediency. And thank you for tying up and tucking in my loose threads.

Many thanks to Karen Anderson for her reading and rereading of my text. Your word insight combined with your impeccable sense of flow helped tweak my story.

Mike Atkins, you continue to keep your creative finger in the writing pot. Thank you for your involvement in my career. Your hallmark of integrity is honorable. It feels safer knowing you're alongside me in the process.

Always and forever a big thank you to my family. You all inspire in ways that would probably surprise you. Danya Clairmont, you realize I would never find anything if I didn't use your resilient mind to keep me on track. Thanks, too, for being a sounding board for my ideas, which I'm sure must seem endless. Left on my own I'm sure I would fill up with the helium of distraction and be found floating somewhere over Narnia.

Jeana, Kyle, Karen, Mike, Danya . . . you are more than you know!

About the Author

Patsy Clairmont is a bookish woman who loves words and has a penchant for dark chocolate sorbet. Since spelling bees in grade school, childhood Scrabble games, right up to her current addiction with Words with Friends she has been known to spell it out, to say it like it is.

Much to her surprise Patsy has written a stack of books that continues to light her passion for the printed page. And nothing pleases her more than to share her faith through laughter and tears and to encourage others to flourish. She has written books in several genres including devotional, fiction, children's, and gift offerings, including bestsellers such as *God Uses Cracked Pots; Normal Is Just a Setting on Your Dryer; I Grew Up Little; All Cracked Up; Catching Fireflies; Kaleidoscope* and more.

A former agoraphobic Patsy never imagined the expansive plans God had in mind for her. She just wanted to make it to her neighborhood grocery store and safely home again. Instead, for the past 35 years she has been traipsing throughout the U.S. and Canada, interspersed with trips to Israel and Africa and she has even spoken at the Pentagon for the Flag Officers Bible Study. Patsy was one of the founding speakers at Women of Faith and trains people for the platform. She has spoken to millions of women (and men) offering spiritual and emotional hope.

Her latest passion is helping people shake loose the stories from their own lives to use in communicating more personally, effectively, and memorably, whether from a stage, a board meeting, a Sunday school class, or over the back fence with a neighbor. We were designed to invest in each other, and sharing our stories is one way to do that.

Patsy and her husband, Les, live in Tennessee.

www.PatsyClairmont.com

Shaking Your Tree
Personal Coaching & Creativity Workshops

You are more than you know and Patsy is eager to tailor a coaching program specifically for you. Would you like to write a book? Share your story from the platform? Find new stories for your already established platform? Or perhaps you'd like to take the next step on attaining a more integrated heart. Patsy will use her extensive experiences in speaking, traveling and writing along with interactive exercises and projects to help you develop creativity and confidence.

Patsy is pleased to offer the Shaking Your Tree program in a number of forms including small group workshops and one-on-one personal coaching.

What others are saying about the *Shaking Your Tree* program:

- *After my weekend in your home, I felt something unleash within myself that felt so comfortable and purposeful.*
- *One of the best experiences I have ever had.*
- *It was a wonderful experience awakening a previously dormant side of me that has been longing to be awakened*

For more information visit:

Patsyclairmont.com/shaking-your-tree

Shaking Your Tree
Small Group Workshops

Through teaching sessions, interactive exercises, and small group activities Patsy helps to stir up the gifts within you. It's her goal to assist as you become a lifelong learner through books, art, and stories. Some of the topics that will be addressed:

- Tap into the rich resources of your history
- Infuse your communications with personality and personalization
- Unleash new levels of creativity adding dynamics to all you do
- Experience a greater sense of inner cohesion
- Creative writing strategies
- How to take your story and put it into book form

These sessions are hosted a number of times a year and are held in Patsy's home in Franklin, TN.

For more information visit:

Patsyclairmont.com/shaking-your-tree

Shaking Your Tree
One-on-One Coaching

This coaching program is a program where Patsy works with you one on one in her home or via video chat. This type of coaching is *completely customized* for you:

- Are you at the beginning of your journey and wondering what your next step is?
- Are you an established speaker or author investigating ways to communicate in a more effective way?
- Are you looking to "shake loose" your story in a safe environment?

Patsy will sit alongside you as you work through these areas together through:

- Material Evaluation (identifying your voice)
- Brainstorming (strengthening your style)
- Personalized Planning…that fits your life   (ongoing self-education)

For more information visit:

Patsyclairmont.com/shaking-your-tree

Rosecreek Road
Patsy's Studio

I just opened an online art studio. Even as I type the words I am freshly taken a-back by God's kindness. I thought I'd like to own a bookstore or a gift shop, but art store? No, I'm not the type. Oh, the desire to dib and dab on a canvas has been there since childhood, but not any "seen" results. My painterly longing didn't know how to find its way out of my desire...

until...

An art class 2 years ago. I took it almost as a lark only to find the art teacher was as quirky as me and she coaxed my artsy heart by giving me permission to find my style. And what I found is I'm a whimsical artist, in that I love layering paint, building texture, and surprise, surprise, my pieces are quite playful and full of attitude.

To my even greater surprise people began asking if they could buy copies of some of my paintings...thus "Rosecreek Road." The name came from my mother's childhood so it pleases me to incorporate her history into my studio.

I'd be so delighted to have you visit Rosecreek Road and peruse my latest creative effort. You might see an owl who grew up to be a rubber duck, a wacky chicken full of attitude or a cow who has her moo on.

Keep your personal options for new growth open, you have no idea what God has in store for you! You are more than you know...because God is greater than you can imagine.

RosecreekRoad.com